Trevor and Duncan Smith are father and son respectively and this is their first co-written work.

Trevor Smith, of Scottish extraction, was born in Sheffield in 1921. He has had a varied career, including some eight years of teaching and many more in public and University libraries. He has a lifelong interest in freelance writing and photography and for some considerable time has been completing a list of curiosities of the British Isles.

Duncan Smith, now 31, was born and raised in Sheffield. From the age of 10 he has been a keen collector of all things historical, going on to read ancient history and archaeology at Birmingham University. A keen traveller, gardener and book-collector, he currently works in the publishing industry.

Frontispiece
W... folly chimney at Halifax (see No 62).

South and West Yorkshire Curiosities

Duncan and Trevor Smith

THE DOVECOTE PRESS

For Mary, Catherine, Adrian and Eva

First published in 1992 by The Dovecote Press Ltd
Stanbridge, Wimborne, Dorset BH21 4JD

ISBN 0 946159 99 8

© Duncan and Trevor Smith 1992

Phototypeset in Times by The Typesetting Bureau Ltd
Wimborne, Dorset
Printed and bound in Singapore

Contents

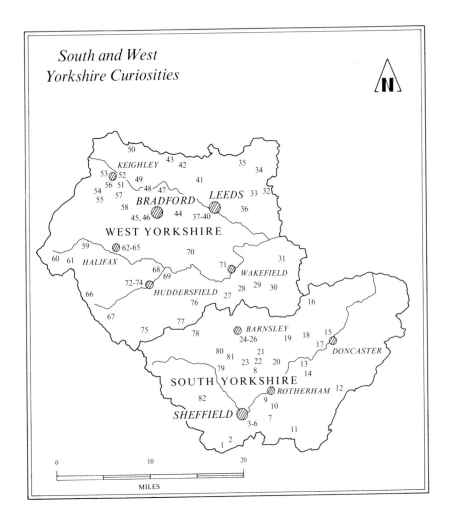

South and West Yorkshire Curiosities

Introduction

The term "curiosity" is of necessity a subjective one. The criteria adopted here are that it be not necessarily unique but certainly rare, and that it be historically or architecturally unusual. It can be important or trivial, famous or little known, but it must have an interesting story behind it which evokes bygone days in Yorkshire.

Our journey will take us from prehistoric times right through to the present day, and from one end of the county to the other. We shall visit moors littered with early man's remains, travel along old packhorse ways and through quiet country house estates, see the once bustling textile mills of the west and the noisy iron and steel furnaces of the south, many now silent. One moment we will be in sleepy villages, parks and churchyards, and the next in busy city centres with their railways, roads and canals, touching on the age-old Yorkshire themes of beer and cricket as we go. We shall also encounter eccentric characters and their follies, as well as the tangible remains of some of our more curious customs.

In a county as large as ours, with its many major centres of population, it has been necessary to limit the scope of this present volume to the south and west, comprising as it does much of the old West Riding. Even then our choice is an arbitrary one, limited to sites which are visible and visitable in order to produce a practical guide-book. This we hope will engender an affection for the more unusual sites around us and thereby encourage people to visit and protect them.

Many of the sites described can be seen easily all year round. Others, however, are stately homes and museums with opening hours and admission prices. The odd one is even on private land in which case permission must always be sought. In the case of churches, it is best to visit on Sundays as many are now sadly locked during the week.

Directions have been kept brief and all map references refer to the Ordnance Survey 1:50,000 Landranger series. A glance at our map will show that the sites are numbered in a broadly anti-clockwise direction beginning in Sheffield. At the end of each entry is a selection of other sites described in the book which lie within a five mile radius. Occasionally, as is the case with curious graves and ancient wells, a number of examples are brought together from all around the area forming a thematic journey in itself.

Duncan and Trevor Smith
Sheffield, 1992.

Acknowledgements

Many people have helped us in the compilation of this book and we would like to express our thanks to the following.

First and foremost David Burnett of The Dovecote Press for his enthusiasm and for giving us the chance to publish our work. Also Simon Laffoley, for his companionship on many journeys into the field and his invaluable help with map-reading, and to Jane Wood for typing the manuscript.

Among the friendly and helpful people we encountered at many of the sites: Stanley Clarke (Hemingfield), Tom Beastall (Tickhill), Richard Van Riel and Julie Loftus (Pontefract), Mrs D Kaye (Walton), Mrs Denton (Denby Dale), Mr J R Griffiths (Gunthwaite), Alan Blakeman (Elsecar), Mr B Lockyear (Sheffield), Olga Martin (Aston) and Mrs Hazel Wragg (Bradfield).

For permission to take photographs: The National Trust (Nostell Priory), English Heritage (Conisbrough Castle and Monk Bretton Priory), Pauline Beswick of Sheffield City Museums (Sheffield Manor).

For permission to use existing photographs: Cambridge University Committee for Aerial Photography and the Ministry of Defence (Bentley Grange), John Hislop (Hemingfield), and John Morrison (Blackstone Edge Roman Road from *Pennine Rails and Trails*, 1990). For permission to use illustrations: Martin Rigg for an old engraving of Sheffield, and David Higham Associates for a drawing of the Adel sanctuary knocker published in *A Guide to Norman Sites in Britain* (Granada) by Nigel and Mary Kerr.

Special thanks are extended to Rob Wilson for the use of material relating to ancient wells as published in his book *Holy Wells and Spas of South Yorkshire* (1991).

Finally, thanks to the following who were more than happy to spare a few minutes talking about this book: Andrew Sharpe, Jonathan Schofield, Tim Broadley, Elaine Beardsell, Gordon Bowers and our family and friends.

KING ECGBERT OF WESSEX
LED HIS ARMY TO DORE
IN THE YEAR A·D 829
AGAINST KING EANRED
OF NORTHUMBRIA
BY WHOSE
SUBMISSION
KING ECGBERT
BECAME FIRST
OVERLORD
OF ALL
ENGLAND

1 England's First King

Position: Dore (S.Yorks)
O.S.Map: Sheffield & Huddersfield Area Sheet: 110
Map Ref: SK 309/811
Access: Dore lies on the A621, 5 miles south-west of Sheffield. The village green is reached along Dore Road, opposite the railway station, and left along Vicarage Lane.

On the village green can be found a sandstone monolith on which is attached a plaque in the shape of a Saxon shield. This records the fact that it was here in A.D.829 that King Ecgbert of Wessex received the submission of King Eanred of Northumberland, thereby becoming first overlord of all England. Until this date England had been dominated by the three warring Saxon royal dynasties of Northumbria, Mercia and Wessex. Both the former came close to gaining overlordship of England but it was the king of the west Saxon house of Wessex, Ecgbert, who finally unified Anglo-Saxon England.

Ecgbert, whose name means "Bright Sword", reigned from 802-839 A.D. and gained a wider supremacy than any of his predecessors. Northumbria, however, remained aloof and the Anglo-Saxon Chronicle records how Ecgbert led his army into Dore, on the Mercian-Northumbrian border, where King Eanred surprisingly submitted without a fight. It is thought that Northumbria was being ravaged by Scandinavian invaders at the time, forcing Eanred to assist in the consolidation of England into one strong kingdom able to resist them. This ultimately happened under Ecgbert's grandson, Alfred the Great. The plaque also depicts the Golden Dragon of Wessex which was Ecgbert's tribal emblem.

Should you visit Dore in July the old Derbyshire custom of "Well-Dressing" can be observed at the nearby Peace Well. This pre-Christian custom flourishes in Derbyshire and reflects the fact that Dore, until recently, was part of that county.

Places of Interest in the Neighbourhood
2. Sheffield's Industrial Heritage (Sheffield)
3. From Donkey Boy to Sculptor (Sheffield)
4. Sheffield's Garden of Curiosities (Sheffield)
5. Street Lamps of the Past (Sheffield)

The plaque on Dore village green.

2 Sheffield's Industrial Heritage

Position: Sheffield (S. Yorks)
O. S. Map: Sheffield & Doncaster Area Sheet: 111
Map Ref: SK326/820
Access: Abbeydale Industrial Hamlet is on the south-western outskirts of Sheffield on the A621 Abbeydale Road to Bakewell. It is open most days with several working days through the year.

The Abbeydale Industrial Hamlet is perhaps the best preserved working site of crucible or cast steel manufacture in the world. The method was invented by Benjamin Huntsman (1704-1776). Clay crucibles were filled with broken blister steel and lime, melted, and poured into moulds. It was then sent to a rolling mill elsewhere and reduced to one-inch square sections. This was then sent back to Abbeydale, reheated, hammered or milled, and forged to produce scythe blades. They were sharpened on water-powered grindstones, although steam was used during droughts. The tilt-hammers date from 1785 and the grinding shop from 1817, and on working days the water-powered machinery is set into action.

At one time there were many small water-powered grinding shops along Sheffield's valleys. A good example is the Shepherd Wheel (SK317/854), a restored "Little Mester's" cutlery grinding shop off Hangingwater Road in Whiteley Woods, in the Nether Green district. It dates from the late 1500's.

Sheffield's industrial history is fully charted in the Kelham Island Industrial Museum (SK353/883) north of the city centre on Alma Street. Incidentally, the City Museum (SK337/873) on Western Bank near the University boasts the world's best collection of cutlery. For those interested in the city's more recent history, a series of informative blue plaques are being mounted on the remains of important industrial buildings in the east end.

Another rare curiosity is Wilson's 1737 snuff mill (SK339/858) at the top of Sharrowvale Road in the Sharrow district. Still in private hands, much of the original water-powered machinery is in use and the snuff formula is still a family secret.

Places of Interest in the Neighbourhood
3. From Donkey Boy to Sculptor (Sheffield)
4. Sheffield's Garden of Curiosities (Sheffield)
5. Street Lamps of the Past (Sheffield)
6. One of Mary Queen of Scots' Prisons (Sheffield)

3 From Donkey Boy to Sculptor

Position: Sheffield (S. Yorks)
O. S. Map: Sheffield & Huddersfield Area Sheet: 110
Map Ref: SK359/822
Access: Norton is now a suburb of Sheffield, on the A61, south of the city centre. The obelisk is next to the church on Norton Lane.

A monument to Sir Francis Leggott Chantrey (1781-1841) is in Norton Church and a 22 feet obelisk in his honour is beside the road. In fact Norton and its environs are known colloquially as "Chantreyland".

Chantrey was born at Jordanthorpe, the son of a carpenter. He became a grocer's boy in Sheffield, and delivered milk by donkey cart from Norton to the city. He was then apprenticed to a wood-carver from 1797-1802. He studied sculpture and other art forms and became a portrait painter in Sheffield in 1802. He then moved to London, painting portraits and working on his wood-carvings. A very talented painter, he finally exhibited at the Royal Academy (1804-7) but worked mainly as a sculptor. He exhibited statues in 1809, and did a portrait bust of King George IV for which he was paid 300 guineas in 1822.

Perhaps his best known works are his busts of children, and the one of

Norton Church and Chantrey's obelisk.

Satan (suggested by *Paradise Lost*) as well as the sleeping children tomb in Lichfield Cathedral. He made a bequest of £150,000 to the Royal Academy for the purchase of pictures for the nation. This collection is in the Tate Gallery. Chantrey was knighted in 1835 and buried in Norton church.

The Obelisk is sited on the once extensive green and was designed by his friend Philip Hardwick R. A. It was brought by sea to Hull from Cornwall, being made of Cornish granite and was erected in 1854.

Places of Interest in the Neighbourhood
1. England's First King (Dore)
2. Sheffield's Industrial Heritage (Sheffield)
4. Sheffield's Garden of Curiosities (Sheffield)
5. Street Lamps of the Past (Sheffield)
6. One of Mary Queen of Scots' Prisons (Sheffield)

Victorian bear-pit in the Botanical Gardens, Sheffield.

4 Sheffield's Garden of Curiosities

Position: Sheffield (S. Yorks)
O. S. Map: Sheffield & Doncaster Area Sheet: 111
Map Ref: SK336/862
Access: The Botanical Gardens are to the west of the city centre on Clarkehouse Road off the A57.

Near to the main gateway of Sheffield's Victorian Botanical Gardens are the Paxton Greenhouse Pavilions, three miniature Crystal Palaces in cast iron and glass built in 1837.

Beyond on a hillock is the Victorian bearpit. A deep, stone-lined cylinder in the ground, it is surrounded by an iron fence and parapet. Looking over one can detect a stone floor (when it is not leaf-strewn) and there are entrances at the bottom. Bears were kept in this miserable way for the safety of the public. It has been said that bear baiting was carried on in the city at one time, but it seems likely that the bear pit was for displaying the captive animals only.

Straight ahead through the main gates can be found the fossilised stump of a tree, the oldest found in the area. It is thought to be 300 million years old! It was dug up during coal mining on the site of the railway station and was moved to its present location in order to preserve it.

Adjacent is the Crimean War memorial which originally stood at Moorhead in the city centre. The statue of Victory once topped a pillar but this was cut up and now adorns a children's playground in Hammond Street!

Places of Interest in the Neighbourhood
1. England's First King (Dore)
2. Sheffield's Industrial Heritage (Sheffield)
3. From Donkey Boy to Sculptor (Sheffield)
5. Street Lamps of the Past (Sheffield)
6. One of Mary Queen of Scots' Prisons (Sheffield)

5 Street Lamps of the Past

Position: Sheffield (S. Yorks)
O. S. Map: Sheffield & Doncaster Area Sheet: 111
Map Ref: SK346/872
Access: The street lamp is on Eldon Street off West Street leading out of the city centre towards the University.

Sheffield has a number of sewer gas lamps which are more accurately called "J. E. Webb Patent Sewer Gas Destructors"! Dating from the nineteenth-century and designed to minimise the danger of explosion from methane gas building up in the sewers, they were a Birmingham invention.

Those in Sheffield were put up between 1914 and 1935. Thanks to the efforts of a Sheffield schoolboy and his friends, and the interest of a local postman, there are still 19 or so well-tended survivors out of the original 82.

Places of Interest in the Neighbourhood
1. England's First King (Dore)
2. Sheffield's Industrial Heritage (Sheffield)
3. From Donkey Boy to Sculptor (Sheffield)
4. Sheffield's Garden of Curiosities (Sheffield)
6. One of Mary Queen of Scots' Prisons (Sheffield)

One of Sheffield's sewer gas lamps.

6 One of Mary Queen of Scots' Prisons

Position: Sheffield (S. Yorks)
O. S. Map: Sheffield & Doncaster Area Sheet: 111
Map Ref: SK 375/865
Access: Sheffield Manor is on Manor Lane approached from City
Road, the A616 Sheffield to Newark, or take the Manor Park exit off
the M1/City link road known as the Parkway. It is open much of the
year but is also clearly visible from the road.

The Turret House is the only surviving roofed portion of Sheffield
Manor. Originally, in the sixteenth-century, the Manor was a hunting lodge owned by the Talbots, Earls of Shrewsbury. It was visited
by Cardinal Wolsey and later by Mary Queen of Scots, one of the
many places in which she was held imprisoned. George, sixth Earl of
Shrewsbury, and his wife, the famous Bess of Hardwick, were in charge
of her for 14 years both here and at Sheffield Castle, apart from brief

The Turret House at Sheffield Manor.

visits to Buxton, Chatsworth and Worksop. A large part of the Manor was pulled down in 1708 and Sheffield Castle no longer exists except for a fragment hidden in the basement of Castle Market, having been virtually destroyed in 1648.

The Turret House itself could have constituted the gate-house and hunting tower. It dates from 1574, during Mary's captivity, but may have been built specially to house her. It contains an exhibition about the unfortunate queen.

Places of Interest in the Neighbourhood
2. Sheffield's Industrial Heritage (Sheffield)
3. From Donkey Boy to Sculptor (Sheffield)
4. Sheffield's Garden of Curiosities (Sheffield)
5. Street Lamps of the Past (Sheffield)
7. Europe's Oldest Glass Kiln (Catcliffe)

The glass cone at Catcliffe.

7 Europe's Oldest Glass Kiln

Position: Catcliffe (S. Yorks)
O. S. Map: Sheffield & Doncaster Area Sheet: 111
Map Ref: SK425/886
Access: Catcliffe is signposted off the Parkway which links Junction 33
of the M1 with Sheffield city centre. The glass cone can be seen from all
around.

There would appear to have been a very considerable glass industry in
South Yorkshire dating from the early eighteenth-century. The rather
surprising cone at Catcliffe dates from around 1740 and is 60 feet high.
That date makes it the oldest surviving glass cone of its type in Europe.
It is constructed of brick and was once one of a pair.

Originally furnaces were housed in ordinary rectangular shaped buildings but it became the custom to build a cone around the cone-shaped
furnaces. Only another five examples survive in the whole of Britain.
The Catcliffe cone might have been demolished but is fortunately still in
existence. The glassworks were run by William Fenny from the nearby
Bolsterstone works, then by the May family, and by C. Wilcocks & Co.,
among others, and probably ceased manufacture in 1901.

Places of Interest in the Neighbourhood
5. Street Lamps of the Past (Sheffield)
6. One of Mary Queen of Scots' Prisons (Sheffield)
9. Rotherham's Much-used Bridge Chapel (Rotherham)
10. The Castle where Tea Drinking was Forbidden (Rotherham)
11. "Elegy" Written in a Yorkshire Rectory (Aston)

8 Follies Fit for a King

Position: Wentworth (S. Yorks)
O. S. Map: Sheffield & Doncaster Area Sheet: 111
Map Ref: SK395/976
Access: The Wentworth Woodhouse estate lies 4¼ miles north-west of Rotherham on the B6091.

The House at Wentworth Woodhouse is curious in that its east front is the longest country house frontage in England (606 feet). It was built by Thomas Watson-Wentworth, the first Marquess of Rockingham, who had inherited the estate in 1723. The house consists of two fronts in different styles set back-to-back, one of which contains traces of an earlier house built in the 1630's by Sir Thomas Wentworth, one-time minister to Charles I.

Although the house is not yet open to the public, the grounds contain some of the best follies in the county.

Hoober Stand (SK407/986), dating from 1747-49, is a tapering three-sided tower ostensibly commemorating the Battle of Culloden at which the Marquess fought. It just as likely celebrates his elevation by George II from Earl of Malton to Marquess of Rockingham. It stands 1½ miles east of Wentworth village and at 100 feet in height can be seen from all around. Built as a viewing tower, it was claimed York Minster could be seen on a clear day but unfortunately mining subsidence has made it unsafe to climb. A second similar tower of the same period can be seen in Hoyland Nether (SE363/008) at the far end of St Peter's churchyard on the B6096. It was originally built with its own bowling green.

Keppel's Column (SK389/947) is 115 feet high and stands beside the A629, 3 miles north-west of Rotherham. It was begun in 1776 by Charles Watson Wentworth, the Second Marquess of Rockingham and finished in 1782 after his death. It was erected as a protest against the court-martial of Rockingham's friend Viscount Keppel following the naval defeat at the Battle of Ushant in 1778. Keppel was later acquitted, having been used as a scapegoat by corrupt politicians who deprived him of money needed to repair his ships.

The Needle's Eye (SK396/988; see front cover) is probably the strangest of all the follies and has been variously dated between 1730 and 1780. It takes the form of a 48 feet high tapering obelisk pierced by a narrow archway at the base. The story runs that it was erected by the second Marquess to win a bet that he could not drive his coach and horses through the eye of a needle! It is situated on top of a ridge on the edge of Lee Wood, off Coaley Lane down an unmarked track by the side of a solitary house.

The Second Marquess died in 1782 having been Prime Minister twice and is interred in a three-storeyed mausoleum (SK414/971) just outside Nether Haugh on the B6091 to Wentworth. It was completed in 1791 by his nephew and heir Earl Fitzwilliam and contains a statue of the Marquess surrounded by busts of his friends. Recently renovated, after coal mining had caused it to subside, it is open on Wednesdays and Sundays in the summer.

Finally, adjacent to the Garden Centre just south of Wentworth village can be found the unexpected remains of an early nineteenth-century Japanese garden (SK389/975). Round every corner can be found mock Roman statues, headless heraldic beasts, grottoes and at the far end an elaborately decorated portal to a seventeenth-century bear-pit. In addition, the estate is dotted with architecturally striking lodges, stables and gate-houses plus a couple of converted windmills with mock crenellations.

Places of Interest in the Neighbourhood

The Needle's Eye folly at Wentworth.

21

9 Rotherham's Much-used Bridge Chapel

Position: Rotherham (S. Yorks)
O. S. Map: Sheffield & Doncaster Area Sheet: 111
Map Ref: SK428/931
Access: Rotherham lies 6 miles north of Sheffield and the chapel is opposite the railway station on Bridge Street.

Of only four surviving bridge, or chantry, chapels in England, two are in Yorkshire. One is at Wakefield (see no. 71) the other is here in Rotherham. This remarkable survival dates back to 1483 and is situated on the original four-arched bridge over the River Don. The bridge was widened in the eighteenth-century and narrowed back to its old width two centuries later.

The chapel itself was asked for in the will of the master of the grammar school, John Bokyng, who left a small amount towards its fabric. It is possible that Archbishop Thomas Rotherham, Archbishop of York, bore the cost of its construction. A light was lit in the chapel every night to guide travellers into Rotherham. It was closed in 1547 by the Act of Dissolution of the Colleges and Chantries. It may have been used, as was Wakefield's, to house people suspected of infection in the days of the plague and was definitely used as an almshouse. In 1779 it became the town lock-up or jail, known locally as "The Jail Bridge", and in 1888 as a tobacconist's and newsagent's. In the twentieth-century it reverted to being a place of worship again and the Bishop of Sheffield dedicated it in 1924 after it had been restored.

Its west front is much less decorated than Wakefield's, and its interior is plain, although the building is battlemented and there is a crypt.

Places of Interest in the Neighbourhood
7. Europe's Oldest Glass Kiln (Catcliffe)
8. Follies Fit for a King (Wentworth)
10. The Castle where Tea Drinking was Forbidden (Rotherham)
20. Clink! (Wath-upon-Dearne)

One of Yorkshire's two bridge chapels, at Rotherham.

10 The Castle where Tea Drinking was Forbidden

Position: Rotherham (S. Yorks)
O. S. Map: Sheffield & Doncaster Area Sheet: 111
Map Ref: SK430/916
Access: Boston Park is a mile south of Rotherham overlooking the Rother Valley. Leave M1 at junction 33 along the A630/631 Wickersley road and turn left along the A618.

Boston Castle is in reality a square, battlemented shooting lodge erected in 1775 by the Earl of Effingham to celebrate the Boston Tea Party. At this time there was considerable sympathy amongst the Whig aristocracy for the American colonies' struggle against the Crown and the Earl resigned his commission rather than fight the colonists. Tea drinking is even said to have been forbidden at the castle's housewarming.

Later, in 1875, the castle and its 22 acre grounds were established as Rotherham's first public park, being rented by the local corporation for £50 a year. Known originally as Rotherham, or The People's Park, it included a "a Lovers' Dale" complete with discreetly placed benches, as well as bowling, croquet and cricket facilities. It was opened on the centenary of the Declaration of Independence on 4th July 1876.

Over the years Boston Park, as it was later known, has become a resting place for fragments of demolished local buildings, most notably the doorway from Jesus College founded in 1483 by Thomas Rotherham. Also to be seen is the Sheffield and Rotherham Railway coat-of-arms from Westgate station and a millstone from a windmill which once stood on Percy Street.

Places of Interest in the Neighbourhood
   6. One of Mary Queen of Scots' Prisons (Sheffield)
   7. Europe's Oldest Glass Kiln (Catcliffe)
   8. Follies Fit for a King (Wentworth)
   9. Rotherham's Much-used Bridge Chapel (Rotherham)
  11. "Elegy" Written in a Yorkshire Rectory (Aston)

11 "Elegy" Written in a Yorkshire Rectory

Position: Aston (S. Yorks)
O. S. Map: Sheffield & Doncaster Area Sheet: 111
Map Ref: SK467/853
Access: Aston is a village 5 miles east of Sheffield on the A57 and the rectory is adjacent to All Saints Church on Church Lane.

The Georgian rectory at Aston was once home to the Rev. William Mason. As well as being a man of the cloth he was also a talented writer and musician and was a friend of the great eighteenth-century poet Thomas Gray. The latter used to come up to visit him and they would talk about each other's work. In fact it was curiously enough in the summer house here that "Scroddles", the nickname given by Gray to his friend, and he discussed a long poem by Gray which became one of the most loved of English poems – "An Elegy Written in a Country Churchyard". The churchyard in question was that of Stoke Poges in Buckinghamshire. Mason made a significant change to the poem by suggesting it be shortened by a few stanzas. Some of the omitted lines were subsequently written over the doorway of the summer house. Although it has since been demolished, busts of the two friends which once adorned its walls can be found inside All Saints church next door.

Places of Interest in the Neighbourhood
 7. Europe's Oldest Glass Kiln (Catcliffe)
10. The Castle where Tea Drinking was Forbidden (Rotherham)

Boston Castle in Rotherham.

12 Yorkshire's Renaissance Superlative

Position: Tickhill (S. Yorks)
O. S. Map: Sheffield & Doncaster Area Sheet: 111
Map Ref: SK592/931
Access: Tickhill is a village about 10 miles east of Rotherham on the A631.

Tickhill is a pleasant village with a fine Georgian pillared market cross, or shelter, known as the "Rotunda". This is circular in plan and was erected in 1777 in the centre of the village. Close by is a ruined castle on a Norman site, once one of the finest fortifications in the north of England, though you would not think so now.

Tickhill's principal beauty, however, is in the church of St Mary. It consists of an alabaster altar-tomb which is considered to be the finest monument in the Italian Renaissance style in the country. Dating from about 1530 the tomb chest bears the effigies of Thomas Fitzwilliam and his first wife Elizabeth. Its design resembles Torrigiani's tomb of Henry VII with a shield held by 2 cherubs.

In front of the church stands a row of recently constructed almshouses. These have been rebuilt many times and are believed to have been founded by John of Gaunt.

Places of Interest in the Neighbourhood
No sites lie within a 5 mile radius of Tickhill.

The Norman keep at Conisbrough Castle.

13 Ivanhoe's Castle

Position: Conisbrough
O. S. Map: Sheffield & Doncaster Area Sheet: 111
Map Ref: SK 515/989
Access: Conisbrough Castle is north-east of the town centre, off the
A630, 4½ miles south-west of Doncaster, off the A1(M). It is an
English Heritage property open all year round.

Conisbrough Castle has one of the oldest and finest Norman cylindrical
keeps in Britain. Its founder, William de Warenne, was created first
Norman Earl of Surrey and given the land around Conisbrough by
William the Conqueror in recognition of his assistance in the conquest
of England. A mound was made and topped by a wooden palisade.
Later, Hamelin Plantagenet married Isabel de Warenne and started the
stone keep around 1180. It is 90 feet high with six huge buttresses and is
surrounded by a curtain wall. Part of this and part of the barbican have
unfortunately begun to slip into the moat. In fact there was a collapse
of 60 yards of curtain wall and a gate-tower as early as 1538. A pigeon
loft, oven and two water cisterns existed in the hollows on top of the
buttresses. The existence of wash-basins and latrines show the increas-
ing sophistication of plumbing in castles. The base of the keep projects
so that stones dropped from the walls bounced off onto an enemy.

The castle is a curious reminder of Norman splendour in a small
Yorkshire industrial town. It is also remembered as the imaginary
Saxon castle in Sir Walter Scott's *Ivanhoe*, in which it was the home of
the character Athelstane, a scene being set in the tiny third floor chapel.

Also Norman in date is an extraordinary Norman tomb in nearby St
Peter's church with carved men, dragons and signs of the Zodiac.

Places of Interest in the Neighbourhood
14. Well, Well, Well! (Conisbrough)
15. A Lord Mayor's Parlour (Doncaster)
17. Curious Church Carvings (Sprotborough)
18. An Initial Mystery (Marr)
19. Unusual Churchyard Gateways (Hickleton)

14 Well, Well, Well!

Position: Conisbrough; and see below for others
O. S. Map: Sheffield & Doncaster Area Sheet: 111; and see below for others
Map Ref: SK511/988; and see below for others
Access: Conisbrough is 4½ miles south-west of Doncaster and the town well is beside the church at the top of Castle Hill; and see below for others.

South and west Yorkshire, like other counties, once relied on natural springs and man-made wells for its water supply. Unfortunately the growth of cities in the industrialised north of England has all but obliterated many of these important sites. A few, however, notably those with a sacred or health-giving aspect, have survived to this day.

St James' Well at Midhopestones (110: SK238/995) on the A616, 10 miles north-west of Sheffield, is south Yorkshire's best-preserved holy well. Consisting of a chamber with stone steps, the well is in a field on the north side of a track leading to Midhope Hall. Such wells often have ancient pagan origins, involving ceremonies to placate the water gods. Later they were Christianised and re-dedicated to saints.

Wishing wells also have distant origins, the finest being in Wath Wood near Swinton (111: SK437/989) on the A633, 4 miles north of Rotherham. It consist of a stone chamber, 6 by 8 feet in size, fed by a channel. Another, which is claimed never to freeze or run dry, is in Graves Park at Norton (110/111: SK354/821) off the A6102, 3 miles south of Sheffield city centre. It is on a path on the south side of a stream flowing through Waterfall Wood, near the boating lake.

Certain wells and springs contained water said to have healing qualities which often proved lucrative for the owner. These were called spas, or "spaws" in the north of England (see also no. 78). The spa at Guilthwaite (111: SK441/883) off the A631, 3 miles south of Rotherham, was discovered in 1664. A bathhouse was hastily built and advertised, and the stone surround and headstone are still visible. Sores and ulcers were cured here, as well as several documented cases of hair restoration!

The most impressive commercial spa to survive is Birley Spa at Hackenthorpe (111: SK409/836), 4 miles south-east of Sheffield. Stone age implements found in the area suggest an ancient origin for these tonic waters. The present building, Birley Spa House, was built in the 1840s and contains a huge bath 25 by 18 feet in size and 6 feet deep. Although

The well-head building at Conisbrough.

it was closed during the Second World War, it remains a listed building and there are plans to create a tourist attraction here.

Another spa, notable for the famous abbey nearby, is Monk's Well at Beauchief (110: SK331/814) off the A621, 4 miles south-west of Shef-field city centre. The well lies down some steps in a wood on the left-hand side of the drive leading from the Abbey up to Beauchief Hall. The waters still drip into a trough and were once claimed to be the country's finest cure for alcoholic ailments.

Finally, there are the purely practical wells which provided a town's water supply, as at Conisbrough (see above for access). Here, the well-head was kept cool and secure by means of a sturdy stone building with a steeply pitched stone roof. At the bottom of Dunford Road in the Underbank area of Holmfirth (110: SE143/082), 5 miles south of Huddersfield, is the "Pump Hole", a town pump and trough sheltered by a stone arch erected in 1850. Further along, on Well Lane (110: SE147/047) is a second town well with water that hasn't ceased flowing in 250 years!

For wells associated with Robin Hood see no. 16.

15 A Lord Mayor's Parlour

Position: Doncaster (S. Yorks)
O. S. Map: Sheffield & Doncaster Area Sheet: 111
Map Ref: SE575/033
Access: Leave the A1 along the A630 into Doncaster town centre, and the Mansion House is on High Street, opposite Scot Lane.

The finest public building in Doncaster is the Civic Mansion House which is one of only 3 such buildings in the country, the others being in London and York. It was commenced in 1744 and the main building finished in 1748. It was from a design by James Paine with additions by William Lindley in 1801-6, who added the attic.

Built as the residence of the Mayor, his parlour is on the ground floor. It is used for meetings of the town council but is also the venue for social functions of the town and district, and has hosted many grand occasions during the race week. The St Leger dinner still takes place here in the Banqueting Hall.

The Mansion House is a three-storeyed stone building, well-known to travellers on the Great North Road. The entrance has 2 pairs of Ionic columns, the columns being placed behind one another. However, the exterior gives little idea of the spaciousness inside. The columned entrance leads to the handsome grand staircase. The first floor boasts a large ballroom and banqueting hall and has exquisitely designed ceilings and fireplace. Lindley added a new Banqueting Hall in 1806, which is at the rear and is one of the finest in the country.

The Municipal treasure here includes the Corporate Plate and Regalia, and the Mace and Mayoral chain. Full-length paintings of local luminaries of the last two centuries join those of royalty such as King George III and Queen Victoria.

Places of Interest in the Neighbourhood
13. Ivanhoe's Castle (Conisbrough)
14. Well, Well, Well! (Conisbrough)
17. Curious Church Carvings (Sprotborough)
18. An Initial Mystery (Marr)

16 Robin Hood's Well

Position: Burghwallis (S. Yorks)
O. S. Map: Sheffield & Doncaster Area Sheet: 111
Map Ref: SE 519/119
Access: The well lies at one end of a lay-by on the south bound A1 between Doncaster and Pontefract just after the Burghwallis turn off.

The area of Barnsdale which surrounds Burghwallis was once densely wooded and a favourite haunt of outlaws, notably Robin Hood. His chief offence in Barnsdale was the baiting of the Bishop of Hereford, the outlaws dressed as shepherds having outnumbered the Bishop's men. He was forced to have a meal of venison with the outlaws before being robbed of £300 to pay for the pleasure. As entertainment, the Bishop was made to dance around a tree with his boots on until exhausted. The well which marked this spot has been known as Robin Hood's Well since the reign of Henry VIII. By 1711 a squat arched stone structure designed by Vanburgh had been erected here by the Earl of Carlisle. The well was once a popular stopping place in the coaching days between York and London and the Robin Hood Inn, which once stood here, boasted a three-pint leather bottle said to have belonged to Robin.

   The well building was carefully moved to its present site from the north side of the Skell stream when the A1 was widened, the well itself having been contaminated years earlier.

Places of Interest in the Neighbourhood
18. An Initial Mystery (Marr)
19. Unusual Churchyard Gateways (Hickleton)

Robin Hood's Well at Burghwallis.

17 Curious Church Carvings

Position: Sprotborough
O. S. Map: Sheffield & Doncaster Area Sheet: 111
Map Ref: SE539/021
Access: Sprotborough lies 2½ miles west of Doncaster, off the A1 at Warmsworth.

The ancient parish church of St Mary's at Sprotborough is well worth a visit for its many curious carvings which remain open to interpretation.

Of great interest is a stone seat, dug up in the churchyard in the nineteenth century, and thought to be a fourteenth-century "frith stool", or sanctuary seat. Like the one at Beverley Minster in Humberside, use of this seat offered criminals a period of asylum from legal prosecution. On the front of the seat is carved a strong bearded man, supporting the seat on his head, and on one of the chair arms is what appears to be a demon clutching a spear.

On the door of the pulpit are carved two drinking vessels and what appears to be a book (the Bible?), thus representing a communion scene. However, a more controversial interpretation would be that the book is indeed a pack of cards and the two vessels a dice-jug and a beer-mug!

The sixteenth-century wooden benches in the nave have carved end-panels depicting male profiles, a curious severed serpent's head and a three-faced man. There is also a couple kissing each other on one bench but facing away on another. Some say this is a couple before and after marriage! In the stalls of the chancel can be found a "misericord". This is a hinged seat which when lifted up reveals an often grotesque carving which affords some support to a standing person. In this case the carving takes the form of a demon, half goat, half horned devil, holding a three-pronged hook.

The clock over the organ always stands at about 5 past 1, said to be the time of death in 1709 of the organ's benefactor, Sir Godfrey Copley, of Sprotborough Hall.

Places of Interest in the Neighbourhood

18 An Initial Mystery

Position: Marr (S. Yorks)
O. S. Map: Sheffield & Doncaster Area Sheet: 111
Map Ref: SE515/053
Access: Marr lies 5 miles north-west of Doncaster on the A635 Barnsley road.

The Church of St Helen of Marr has a fourteenth-century tower but also some Norman herringbone brickwork, so it is of considerable antiquity. It has also a certain amount of wall painting and funeral armour, and the initials ("C. B.") on the pulpit.

It is widely believed, though Pevsner in his book *The Buildings of England* strongly disagrees, that they are those of Christopher Barker, Queen's Printer to Queen Elizabeth I. He is famous for printing many editions of the Bible, including the first edition of the Geneva Bible in England, as well as all other religious works and all state printing of the period. He is also credited with being one of the earliest, if not the earliest, printers to use Roman typeface in England.

If the initials are not those of the said Christopher Barker, then whose are they? The mystery remains.

Places of Interest in the Neighbourhood
13. Ivanhoe's Castle (Conisbrough)
14. Well, Well, Well! (Conisbrough)
16. Robin Hood's Well (Burghwallis)
17. Curious Church Carvings (Sprotborough)
19. Unusual Churchyard Gateways (Hickleton)

The pulpit door in St Mary's Church at Sprotborough.

33

19 Unusual Churchyard Gateways

Position: Hickleton (S. Yorks)
O. S. Map: Sheffield & Doncaster Area Sheet: 111
Map Ref: SE483/053
Access: Hickleton is a village 6 miles north-west of Doncaster on the A635.

Most early churchyards were entered via a "lychgate", or corpse gate. They are roofed gateways providing shelter and rest for coffin-bearers while waiting for the priest. Their designs were matters of local choice and pride and no two are alike.

The old church of St Wilfrid at Hickleton has a lychgate which consists of the original south porch of the church relocated in its present position. This is unusual enough but even more so, and what makes it possibly unique amongst lychgates in Britain, is the fact that human skulls are in a niche in the wall behind a barred window. There are three of them and an accompanying inscription reads "Today for me, tomorrow for thee"! Their identity is completely unknown although it was said in 1934 that the then Lord Halifax alone knew who they were. He never revealed the information, however, not even to his son, Lord Irwin.

Another unusual lychgate in our area is that at Wortley (110: SK307/994), 8 miles north of Sheffield on the A629. This contains a stone coffin-table and has "alpha" and "omega" on the gateposts, possibly alluding to the fact that mortals pass this way when baptised and when buried.

Places of Interest in the Neighbourhood
13. Ivanhoe's Castle (Conisbrough)
14. Well, Well, Well! (Conisbrough)
17. Curious Church Carvings (Sprotborough)
18. An Initial Mystery (Marr)
20. Clink! (Wath-upon-Dearne)

The "lych-gate" into St Wilfrid's churchyard at Hickleton.

20 Clink!

Position: Wath-upon-Dearne
O. S. Map: Sheffield & Doncaster Area Sheet: 111
Map Ref: SE434/008
Access: Wath-upon-Dearne is 4 miles north of Rotherham and the lock-up stands in the middle of a new housing estate called Thornhill Place, off Church Street in the town centre.

In bygone days many villages and small towns had their own tiny equivalent of a jail which could hold one or two miscreants overnight. Several survive, but few in Yorkshire, so the constable's lock-up at Wath may be regarded as a curiosity.

The constable in the eighteenth and nineteenth centuries was a man with many responsibilities as well as being on the District Council and a Pension Officer. He was paid, along with the Dog Whipper, who removed stray dogs from the church, by the Church Wardens.

The Wath lock-up is unusual in being unusually large, with two storeys, the lower of which was probably the cell in view of its sturdy masonry.

Places of Interest in the Neighbourhood
8. Follies Fit for a King (Wentworth)
9. Rotherham's Much-used Bridge Chapel (Rotherham)
13. Ivanhoe's Castle (Conisbrough)
19. Unusual Churchyard Gateways (Hickleton)
22. Steam Engines and Lemonade Bottles (Elsecar)

The constable's lock-up at Wath-Upon-Dearne.

21 An Unusual Bee-Shelter

Position: Hemingfield (S. Yorks)
O. S. Map: Sheffield & Doncaster Area Sheet: 111
Map Ref: SE395/016
Access: Hemingfield is a village 4 miles south-east of Barnsley off the
A633, adjacent to Wombwell.

In olden times many farms kept a colony of bees for the production of
honey. They were housed in conical straw shelters (or "skeps") which,
unlike today's sturdy wooden hives, required protection from the ele-
ments. One method of achieving this was to build a high wall with
alcoves on the sheltered side in which the skeps were placed. These
alcoves are known as bee-boles after a Scots word for a recess in a wall.
In Yorkshire, however, they are referred to as bee-houses. And to con-
fuse the issue further, the term bee-house outside Yorkshire means a
free-standing structure which housed the hives!

   Until recently, at the end of a private track in the village of
Hemingfield, could be found Skyers Hall Farm. Recently demolished,
only its rubble-filled cellars remain and its garden has been overrun

The lost "Bee-Wall" at Hemingfield.

with weeds. However, close by stood the only bee wall left in South and West Yorkshire. It was thought to be 300 years old and stood 20 feet high. It had brick on one side and stone on the other in which up to 36 alcoves for the hives were incorporated. Plans were made to restore and protect it but unfortunately a gale in the mid 1980's blew it down and nothing of this unique structure remains to be seen. However, for reasons of posterity we have included on the previous page a rare photograph of the wall in all its glory – a lost Yorkshire Curiosity!

Places of Interest in the Neighbourhood
  8. Follies Fit for a King (Wentworth)
20. Clink! (Wath-upon-Dearne)
22. Steam Engines and Lemonade Bottles (Elsecar)
23. Cannon Balls and a Curious Custom (Tankersley)
25. Monuments to Brave Miners (Barnsley)

The Newcomen pump engine at Elsecar coal mine.

22 Steam Engines and Lemonade Bottles

Position: Elsecar (S. Yorks)
O. S. Map: Sheffield & Doncaster Area Sheet: 111
Map Ref: SK387/999
Access: Elsecar lies 8 miles north-east of Sheffield and is signposted
from Junction 36 of the M1. Follow signs marked "Elsecar Heritage"
turning right into Distillery Side. It is an English Heritage site open
most of the year.

A rarity in Elsecar is the only Newcomen steam pumping engine still
"in situ". The building in which it is housed is disguised as a Georgian
domestic building. Installed in 1787 it was probably first used in 1795
and modified in 1836. Rated at 13. 16 horsepower this beam engine
could raise water from the mine workings 130 feet below. Although it
was replaced by electric pumps in 1923 it was brought briefly back
under its original motive power during a power cut. The old pit shaft
can be seen nearby.

The National Bottle Museum housed in Earl Fitzwilliam's private
railway station of 1870 is full of curiosities.

Mr Hiram Codd opened a bottle factory in Barnsley in the nineteenth
century. He was the inventor of the famous Codd's Bottle for carb-
onated drinks which was fitted with a glass marble in the neck, rather
than a cork or stopper. A new slang word was consequently added to
the English language – "codswallop"! Wallop was the name given to the
fizzy drink and also to the wooden tool needed to dislodge the marble
which was held in place by the gas.

The glass industry of Barnsley and South Yorkshire developed an
international importance and was exporting world-wide by the late Victorian period. A glass blower even appears on the Barnsley coat-of-
arms.

Places of Interest in the Neighbourhood
 8. Follies Fit for a King (Wentworth)
20. Clink! (Wath-upon-Dearne)
21. An Unusual Bee-Shelter (Hemingfield)
23. Cannon Balls and a Curious Custom (Tankersley)
25. Monuments to Brave Miners (Barnsley)

23 Cannon Balls and a Curious Custom

Position: Tankersley (S. Yorks)
O. S. Map: Sheffield & Doncaster Area Sheet: 111
Map Ref: SK350/995
Access: Tankersley is 7½ miles north of Sheffield off the M1 at Junction 36. Follow signs to Sheffield then turn right to Tankersley and St Peter's church is on Black Lane.

The fourteenth-century church of St Peter at Tankersley contains some Civil War relics in the form of cannon balls and a bullet. They date from April 1643 when the Earl (later Duke of Newcastle) won a victory over 2,000 Roundheads on Tankersley Moor. This probably lay between the church and Hoyland Common to the north-east. The cannon balls, thought to have been made at Wortley Forge (see no. 79), were discovered in Tankersley Park as was the bullet. The latter was found lodged deep in an ash tree in 1876, and was hollow. Some fancifully suggest it contained poison but more likely it was just a practice bullet.

Another curiosity concerning the church is that once a year the local young people would form a ring around it, clasping hands whilst buglers played on the roof. This is known as embracing or "clipping" the church, from the Old English word "clyppan" (to embrace). Clipping occurs during the feast of St Peter in the second week of July and was introduced in 1926 by Canon Archibald Douglas. It does not occur every year however, and not always on a Sunday. The custom is also observed at Guiseley, near Leeds, and at Painswick in Gloucestershire. All are probably rooted in an ancient pagan rite during which people danced around a sacrificial altar in order to ensure fertility and protection of the flocks.

Places of Interest in the Neighbourhood
  8. Follies Fit for a King (Wentworth)
 21. An Unusual Bee-Shelter (Hemingfield)
 22. Steam Engines and Lemonade Bottles (Elsecar)
 24. A Memorial within a Memorial (Barnsley)
 79. This Forge is the Tops! (Wortley)

24 A Memorial within a Memorial

Position: Barnsley (S. Yorks)
O. S. Map: Sheffield & Doncaster Area Sheet: 111
Map Ref: SE339/052
Access: Locke Park lies about a mile south-west of Barnsley town
centre on the A6133.

The 46 acre Locke Park is a memorial to Joseph Locke, one of
Barnsley's important nineteenth-century figures. Educated at Barnsley
Grammar School he went on to be apprenticed to the great George
Stephenson (of "Rocket" fame) and became an outstanding and
prosperous railway builder in his own right. In 1861 his wife Phoebe
donated the park to the town in his memory where a bronze figure of
Locke still stands today. However, the park is dominated by a 70 feet
high Italianate "belvedere" tower surmounted by a circular wooden hut
giving fine views of the town. This is in memory of Mrs Locke herself,
who died in 1866, and was built by her sister Miss McCreary in 1877.
Her initials "S. M. C." can be seen on the weather-vane and elsewhere.

Places of Interest in the Neighbourhood
21. An Unusual Bee-Shelter (Hemingfield)
23. Cannon Balls and a Curious Custom (Tankersley)
25. Monuments to Brave Miners (Barnsley)
26. The Mixed Fortunes of a Priory (Monk Bretton)
79. This Forge is the Tops! (Wortley)

Mrs Locke's tower in Locke Park at Barnsley.

25 Monuments to Brave Miners

Position: Barnsley (S. Yorks)
O. S. Map: Sheffield & Doncaster Area Sheet: 111
Map Ref: SE360/058
Access: The Kendray Hill monument lies east of Barnsley town centre on the A635 Doncaster road.

The development of industry in south and west Yorkshire was largely facilitated by the existence of coal near the surface along the eastern flanks of the Pennines. Workable seams, or "measures", run from Baildon south through Sheffield and into Derbyshire and Nottinghamshire. Localised surface extraction occurred as early as the fifteenth-century but it was not until the late eighteenth-century that the building of roads and canals made coal an exportable commodity. Once it was discovered that coal could replace charcoal, and that it could fire the new steam engines, mining technology was developed rapidly and the deeper seams to the east were exploited. However, in terms of human life the price of coal extraction was high. On Kendray Hill in Barnsley for example, is a monument to the 361 men and boys killed in an underground explosion at the Old Oaks colliery in 1866. It also records the great courage of John Mammatt and Thomas Embleton who went down to rescue the sole survivor.

   In the churchyard at Darfield (SE419/044) 5 miles further east, are the monuments to the 189 buried alive in the Lundhill Colliery disaster of 1857, and the 10 who died at Houghton Main pit in 1886.

   Finally in All Saints churchyard at Silkstone (SE291/059), 4 miles west of Barnsley on the A628, is a monument to the 26 children who drowned in a flooded pit in 1838.

   Should you wish to experience a Victorian mine first hand visit the Caphouse Yorkshire Mining Museum (SE254/165), on the A642 between Wakefield and Huddersfield.

Places of Interest in the Neighbourhood
21. An Unusual Bee-Shelter (Hemingfield)
22. Steam Engines and Lemonade Bottles (Elsecar)
23. Cannon Balls and a Curious Custom (Tankersley)
26. The Mixed Fortunes of a Priory (Monk Bretton)

The Kendray Hill mining monument in Barnsley.

26 The Mixed Fortunes of a Priory

Position: Monk Bretton (S. Yorks)
O. S. Map: Sheffield & Doncaster Area Sheet: 111
Map Ref: SE373/065
Access: Monk Bretton is 2 miles east of Barnsley town centre, near the junction of the A633 and the A628. The Priory is signposted and is an English Heritage property open all year round.

The ruins of Monk Bretton Priory founded in 1154 by Adam Fitzwaine are unique as being the only Cluniac Order of monks' building in Yorkshire. After an erratic early history including numerous disputes over the appointment of priors, the priory broke away from the Cluniac Order and became an independent Benedictine monastery in 1281. The fortunes of the Priory continued to fluctuate and in 1386 some of the buildings were destroyed by fire. Considerable rebuilding was necessary in the fifteenth century to counter subsidence caused by a geological fault.

The buildings were stripped after the surrendering of the Priory to the King's Commissioners in 1538. Subsequently, in 1546, the north wall of the nave was dismantled, and re-built at Wentworth church and part of the building became a private residence. The largely intact gatehouse is fifteenth-century, and the fourteenth-century guest house has been finely restored. The reredorter, that is the lavatory or main drain, is in an unusually fine state of preservation.

Places of Interest in the Neighbourhood
21. An Unusual Bee-Shelter (Hemingfield)
22. Steam Engines and Lemonade Bottles (Elsecar)
23. Cannon Balls and a Curious Custom (Tankersley)
24. A Memorial within a Memorial (Barnsley)
25. Monuments to Brave Miners (Barnsley)

The main drain at Monk Bretton Priory.

27 The Moving Bridge Chapel

Position: Newmillerdam (W. Yorks)
O. S. Map: Sheffield & Doncaster Area Sheet: 111
Map Ref: SE332/116
Access: The chapel is at Kettlethorpe Hall in Newmillerdam, 3 miles south of Wakefield on the A61, down a track beside the Pledwick Well public house.

Kettlethorpe Hall is a Georgian house famous for the fact that Caroline Norton, granddaughter of the dramatist Sheridan, lived here. She was the author of the famous poem "The Arab's Farewell to his Steed".

When the famous fourteenth-century bridge chapel of St Mary's at Wakefield (see no. 71) was being renovated in 1847, its weathered facade was purchased by the Norton family. It was transferred to Kettlethorpe Hall and re-built on the edge of a lake in the garden. A room built behind it turned it into the curious boat house we see today.

The old frontage of Wakefield's bridge chapel at Kettlethorpe Hall.

28 An Eccentric but Enlightened Squire

Position: Walton (W. Yorks)
O. S. Map: Sheffield & Doncaster Area Sheet: 111
Map Ref: SE364/165
Access: Walton lies 3 miles south-east of Wakefield off the A638
Doncaster road and Walton Hall is signposted beyond.

Walton Hall was once home to one of the most eccentric but oddly
attractive characters to have lived in Yorkshire – the explorer Charles
Waterton (1782-1865). He wrote an account of his global wanderings
and 3 books of natural history essays recording his various adventures.
In South America for example, he hooked and then rode to the river
bank a large crocodile, as well as punching and then capturing a large
boa constrictor. He collected many specimens of snakes, birds and
animals and preserved them by his own innovative form of taxidermy,
examples of which can be found in Wakefield Museum. However, not
all his victims ended up stuffed! He created his own bird sanctuary at
Walton Hall, including a building solely designed to house starlings. A
high wall surrounding the estate was erected to protect all those crea-
tures on the ground and Waterton should be remembered as one of the
first "green" conservationists.

Walton Hall, Island home of naturalist Charles Waterton.

The Palladian hall itself was built by his father Thomas in 1768 and stands on an island in a lake reached by a cast iron bridge. Among the oddities still preserved is a sundial close to the house comprising 20 triangular surfaces giving the time in as many countries. There is also a pair of knockers on the front door, one with a smiling face which doesn't work, and an unhappy one which does knock!

Next to the footbridge on the island is the so-called "Watergate" entrance. This is all that remains of the earlier medieval house whose moat was enlarged into the lake which surrounds the house today.

Despite his renown for strange clothes, Waterton was an enlightened and hospitable man who would invite the inmates of Wakefield Asylum to eat and dance in a now sadly lost grotto in the grounds. The hall was finally sold in 1876 by his son and is now an hotel.

On the hillside opposite the junction of the A638 with the Walton road stands a plain stone tower (SE353/198). Surprisingly this dates from the seventeenth-century and is probably England's earliest water tower. It once supplied the now demolished Heath Old Hall near Wakefield.

Places of Interest in the Neighbourhood
27. The Moving Bridge Chapel (Newmillerdam)
29. Keeping Cool at Nostell Priory (Wragby)
71. The Bridge Chapel of St Mary's (Wakefield)

The Gothic "Menagerie" building at Nostell Priory (© The National Trust 1992).

29 Keeping Cool at Nostell Priory

Position: Wragby (W. Yorks)
O. S. Map: Sheffield & Doncaster Area Sheet: 111
Map Ref: SE404/175
Access: Wragby is 6 miles south-east of Wakefield on the A638
Doncaster road, off which the Priory is signposted. It is a National
Trust property open at weekends only.

Nostell Priory is in fact a Palladian mansion built for the Winn family
on the former site of an Augustinian priory. Construction began in
1735-6 under the supervision of the brilliant Georgian architect James
Paine, then only 19 years old. Robert Adam was responsible for much
of the interior as well as a wing added in 1776. The furniture was the
responsibility of Thomas Chippendale, "the Shakespeare of English
cabinet makers" and is regarded as the finest collection in Britain.

However, it is in the grounds of the house where the true curiosities
are to be found. For instance, the medieval church of St Michael, near
the main entrance (SE407/174), contains a famous collection of Swiss
painted glass.

At the end of a relaxing walk along the lake behind the house can be
found a lush and secret garden set in a hollow. Here lies a secluded
Gothic summer house (or "Menagerie" as it originally housed animal
keepers) where past visitors sought shade and seclusion. There is also a
Gothic alcove in the form of a stone bridge. Nearby, cut into the surrounding sandstone banks can be found an "icehouse", where ice cut in
winter was stored for summer use. Hollowed out of the lawn is a 200-
year-old stepped pit where cockfights were held.

A final curiosity can be viewed by appointment only as it lies on
private land (Telephone Wakefield 862221). This is the northern
gateway to the estate, known as the Pyramid Lodge (SE406/187),
reached along the B6133. It takes the form of a steep-sided pyramid
with an arched entrance cut through it, hence its local name of "The
Needle's Eye".

Places of Interest in the Neighbourhood

30 Memories of the Plague

Position: Ackworth (W. Yorks)
O. S. Map: Sheffield & Doncaster Area Sheet: 111
Map Ref: SE446/187
Access: Ackworth is 3 miles south of Pontefract on the A628 and the plague stone is outside the village on the Pontefract road next to the water tower.

Positioned deliberately on the outskirts of the village of Ackworth is a relic of the plagues which once devastated Britain and Europe. This takes the form of a large stone with a hollowed out basin which once probably contained water and vinegar. Into this the infected villagers placed coins. These coins, thus sterilised, would be picked up by out-siders at a later stage in return for food which they left at the stone. In this way the spread of the plague outside the village was avoided. Though not dated, the stone is thought to date from the plague of 1645 which, according to the great number of deaths recorded in the parish register, was the most serious occurrence.

A rather unusual custom persists at Harvest Festival at Ackworth. The Rector places a sheaf of corn on the staff of an effigy of St. Cuth-bert in the church porch. This is thought to echo an old Norse tradition of hanging out corn for the ravens.

Places of Interest in the Neighbourhood

The Plague Stone at Ackworth.

31 A Little Known but Curious Town

Position: Pontefract (W. Yorks)
O. S. Map: York and surrounding Area Sheet: 105
Map Ref: See below
Access: Pontefract lies 5 miles north-east of Wakefield on the A645.

One of the least known of England's great historical towns, Pontefract, Shakespeare's "Pomfret", owes its existence to a great Medieval castle (SE461/224) which was a major Royalist stronghold in the Civil War. Its underground chambers can still be visited, their walls covered in prisoners' inscriptions.

   Despite much later development, the town retains a good number of curiosities. In the Court Room of the old Town Hall (SE457/219) in Gillygate, accessible from the Assembly Rooms on Bridge Street at the top of Horsefair, is the plaster cast from which one of the four panels was made which surround the base of Nelson's Column. It depicts Nelson mortally wounded on board *The Victory*.

   Beneath Pontefract Hospital (SE458/218) off Southgate can be found

Dupier's Buttercross in Pontefract.

"The Hermitage", founded in 1368 by the hermit Brother Adam. It is reached by 62 steps and comprises an oratory and living room hewn from the solid rock. It is open several times a year (phone the Museum – Pontefract 797289).

Close by is Friarwood Valley Gardens (SE455/215), once home to the Black Friars who arrived here in the thirteenth century from the Mediterranean. Some believe it was they who introduced the herb liquorice to the area which later provided the raw material for the town's famous liquorice industry.

In the Market Place can be seen the Buttercross (SE455/219), a shelter for people selling dairy produce. It was erected in 1734 by the widow of Solomon Dupier who 30 years earlier had been a member of Gibraltar's Spanish garrison. He is thought to have assisted, by betrayal, the Anglo-Dutch force who captured the rock in 1704.

Finally, on Ferrybridge Road, not far from the base of a twelfth-century boundary cross, is "Nevison's Leap". Here Nevison (1639-85), a notorious highwayman, leapt on horseback across the road cutting to escape his pursuers. It was he also, and not Dick Turpin, who achieved the record breaking ride from London to York!

Places of Interest in the Neighbourhood
29. Keeping Cool at Nostell Priory (Wragby)
30. Memories of the Plague (Ackworth)

Sir Thomas Gascoigne's Victory Arch in Parlington Park, Aberford.

32 The Pro-Republican Archway

Position: Aberford (W. Yorks)
O. S. Map: York and surrounding Area Sheet: 105
Map Ref: SE422/365
Access: Parlington Park lies just south of Aberford, off the A1. The arch is on Parlington Drive down the side of the Swan public house.

With the demolition of the house in Parlington Park in 1950 its follies and garden structures became ruinous and neglected. However, still to be seen is the three-arched Triumphal or Victory Arch proclaiming:
  "Liberty. In. N. America. Triumphant. MDCCLXXXIII"
  It was designed by Thomas Leverton for Sir Thomas Gascoigne in 1781 when Cornwallis's surrender brought a successful end to the American Revolution. Gascoigne was an M.P. who had a Pro-Republican ally in the Duke of Norfolk, who built follies at Greystoke in Cumbria also to celebrate rebellion against the crown. However, not everyone sympathised and when the Prince of Wales visited Parlington in 1806 he read the inscription on the arch and promptly turned back. Nearby is a ruinous Gothic building with an arcade of 8 arches which was once a thatched deer shed.
  Also to be seen at Aberford are the Gascoigne almshouses (SE432/364) given by the family in 1844. They are flamboyant for the period with their striking tower, gables and Gothic pinnacles, resembling more a University college than an almshouse.

Places of Interest in the Neighbourhood
33. The Tallest Maypole (Barwick-in-Elmet)
34. A Yorkshire Versailles (Bramham)
35. A Pub in the Record Book (Bardsey)

33 The Tallest Maypole

Position: Barwick-in-Elmet (W. Yorks)
O. S. Map: Leeds, Bradford & Harrogate Area Sheet: 104
Map Ref: SE399/375
Access: Barwick lies 6 miles east of Leeds city centre on the A64 and the maypole dominates the village square.

The practice of raising a maypole in Barwick-in-Elmet has strong and ancient traditions. When the country was covered in forest, tree worship was common and it was customary in spring to go into the woods and cut down a tree. The tree, along with the blessings of the tree spirit, was brought into the village and re-erected, thereby ensuring fertility for crops, cattle and women alike.

With the passing of time these ancient origins blurred and the maypole became a permanent fixture which was decorated with flowers during May Day festivities. Despite the custom being banned by the Puritans it was restored under Charles II. By this time the custom had taken on a new role as a symbol of village independence, inter-village feuds often developing as villagers sought to cut down and steal each others' maypole.

In Barwick-in-Elmet the post is lowered every 3 years on Spring Bank Holiday requiring 150 men with ropes and ladders. At 88 feet 6 inches it is the highest pole in the country. Floral garlands are taken around neighbouring villages and donations collected. The pole is re-painted red, white and blue and re-erected, accompanied by a procession, the May Queen and, of course, Morris men.

Places of Interest in the Neighbourhood
32. The Pro-Republican Archway (Aberford)
34. A Yorkshire Versailles (Bramham)
35. A Pub in the Record Book (Bardsey)
36. What's in a Name? (Temple Newsam)

34 A Yorkshire Versailles

Position: Bramham (W. Yorks)
O. S. Map: York and surrounding Area Sheet: 105
Map Ref: SE412/418
Access: The village of Bramham is 9 miles east of Leeds just off the A1
between Doncaster and Wetherby. Bramham Park is signposted and is
a National Trust property open between 16th June and 1st September.

The estate at Bramham Park was laid out between 1698 and 1710 by
Robert Benson who, like his father before him, was M. P. and Lord
Mayor of York. The Florentine-style house has been continuously
occupied to the present except for a period of 80 years following a
serious fire in 1828. Benson was also Lord Chamberlain to Queen Anne
who reputedly stayed here. He resigned office, however, in 1713 and was
created Lord Bingley, later going to Spain as Ambassador.

There is little doubt that it was while travelling abroad that he gained
inspiration for the true glory of his estate – the gardens. He visited
the formal gardens designed by the great French Renaissance desig-
ner Le Notre at Louis XIV's palace at Versailles which, although con-
ceived on a far grander scale, influenced the layout of his own garden.
Bramham's famous hedge-lined walks, the Obelisk Pond and the cas-
cades are so like the Frenchman's work that it was once believed he
actually designed them, although in reality he never visited England.
The vistas of magnificent beech hedges lead the eye to two temples
(added 1750-70) and a four-faced urn (representing the four seasons).
This is very typical of the great French gardens of this period and is
thought to be unique in England.

Near the so-called "Gothic Temple" (or "Octagon"), built in 1750 by
Benson's successor as a combined summer-house and water tower, can
be found the graves of the family dogs. The second temple, near the
entrance, is in the classical style built originally as an orangery but now
used as a chapel.

Bingley married Lady Elizabeth Finch, eldest daughter of Lord Ayles-
ford, and had one daughter, Harriet, who succeeded him. Her only son
died young and there is an obelisk in his memory erected in 1763.

Places of Interest in the Neighbourhood
32. The Pro-Republican Archway (Aberford)
33. The Tallest Maypole (Barwick-in-Elmet)
35. A Pub in the Record Book (Bardsey)

35 A Pub in the Record Book

Position: Bardsey
O. S. Map: Leeds, Bradford & Harrogate Area Sheet: 104
Map Ref: SE362/428
Access: Bardsey is on the Leeds to Wetherby road (A58), 8 miles north east of Leeds.

No less an authority than the Guinness Book of Records mentions the Bingley Arms at Bardsey as being the oldest continuously inhabited public house in Britain. It can boast a set of records of brewers and innkeepers dating back to 953 A.D. when Samson Ellis started brewing ale here.

The original building still stands and forms the central part, the wings being added in 1738, although the brew house was destroyed in 1942. It features two priest holes, one in the chimney, used to hide priests who came to give mass to the local gentry after the dissolution of the monasteries. It also has a Dutch oven.

The inn was connected with Kirkstall Abbey and used as a place of rest by monks travelling to St Mary's Abbey at York. The local court was also held here from the eleventh century onwards and offenders were punished in a pillory opposite the church. The inn remained with the Ellis family until 1780 when it was bought by Baron Bingley who changed its name from Priests' Inn to the Bingley Arms.

Bardsey has two further distinctions. One is its church of All Hallows which has a notable Anglo-Saxon tower. Secondly, it was the birthplace of William Congreve (1670-1729), famous for *The Way of the World* and other Restoration plays.

Places of Interest in the Neighbourhood
32. The Pro-Republican Archway (Aberford)
33. The Tallest Maypole (Barwick-in-Elmet)
34. A Yorkshire Versailles (Bramham)

36 What's in a Name?

Position: Temple Newsam (W. Yorks)
O. S. Map: Leeds, Bradford & Harrogate Area Sheet: 104
Map Ref: SE357/322
Access: To reach Temple Newsam Park take the A64 east out of Leeds
then southeast along the A63. The house is signposted down a minor
road.

The name Temple Newsam suggests correctly that here was once the
site of an establishment owned by the Knights Templar. The Newsam
manor had been held by Anglo-Saxons from before the Conquest but
then fell to the De Lacy family. It was they who presented it to the
crusading knights who in turn retained it until Edward II took it following the political disgrace of the Templars in the fourteenth century.

   The building to be seen today was built by Thomas Lord Darcy in
1521. It is said to be haunted by no less than 2 ladies and a murderer.
One of the women is Jane Dudley, who hanged herself on learning
that Lord Darnley had promised to marry Mary Queen of Scots. The
murderer is said to be William Collinson who murdered his mistress,
Phoebe Gray, in 1704 and was hung in York.

Places of Interest in the Neighbourhood
33. The Tallest Maypole (Barwick-in-Elmet)
37. The World's Oldest Railway (Leeds)
38. The Egyptian Linen Mill (Leeds)
39. The Sacrilegious Railway (Leeds)

Haunted Temple Newsam fronted by a brick maze.

37 The World's Oldest Railway

Position: Leeds (W. Yorks)
O. S. Map: Leeds, Bradford & Harrogate Area Sheet: 104
Map Ref: SE303/322
Access: Moor Road Railway station is in Hunslet, south of Leeds city centre, adjacent to the M1.

The growth of Leeds as an industrial centre was founded on its entrepreneurial merchants, abundant supply of coal and a geographical position which favoured the growth of a communication network. Cloth merchants settled here early and rendered the River Aire navigable to the east coast. Small collieries soon sprang up, the coal being taken to waiting barges by horse and cart. However, when Charles Brandling of Gosforth Hall, near Killingworth, inherited estates and collieries at Middleton in 1749 he improved the system. This he did in 1755 by building a wooden horse-drawn waggon-way from Middleton to the Aire at Thwaite Gate. Ultimately he wanted a direct route to the centre of Leeds and to achieve this he sought the first ever Act of Parliament to authorise a railway. Its approval on 9th June 1758 meant the line now went to Casson Close near Leeds Bridge which, together with the opening of the Leeds and Liverpool canal to Skipton, assured the rapid industrialisation of Leeds.

However, by the time of the Napoleonic wars, horse and fodder prices had risen dramatically, prompting engineers John Blenkinsop and Matthew Murray to experiment with steam locomotives. By 1812 the line had become the world's first to be worked by steam on a commercial basis. The new engines running on a metal ratchet railway provided inspiration for George Stephenson's "Rocket".

Although technically the line was soon surpassed, it was not until 1958 that closure was threatened and it became the first standard gauge railway to be preserved by amateurs. Today a three mile steam railway is run along much of the original line at weekends and Bank holidays.

Places of Interest in the Neighbourhood
36. What's in a Name? (Temple Newsam)
38. The Egyptian Linen Mill (Leeds)
39. The Sacrilegious Railway (Leeds)
40. Italian Towers and Moroccan Minarets (Leeds)

Steaming up on the world's oldest railway in Leeds.

38 The Egyptian Linen Mill

Position: Leeds (W. Yorks)
O. S. Map: Leeds, Bradford & Harrogate Area Sheet: 104
Map Ref: SE295/326
Access: The Temple Mill is in the Holbeck area of Leeds on Marshall Street off Water Lane, just south of the railway station.

Prior to the importation of cotton, household items such as sheets and towels were made from linen. Its manufacture from the flax plant was pioneered by John Marshall, a young and diligent Leeds draper. In 1787, at the age of 22, he bought a mill where he perfected his machinery, going on to build his first mill in Holbeck in 1791 at the head of the Leeds-Liverpool canal. Business boomed and his son John joined him in 1816 building a second mill with steam-powered machinery. Finally another son James took over and in 1840 built the

The Egyptian-style linen mill in Holbeck, Leeds.

famous Temple Mill. Unlike its gloomy, multi-storey predecessors, this was a vast, single-storey building with cast-iron frame and flat roof. Glass skylights lit the entire work area and ventilators maintained the temperature. The roof was damp-proofed with tar and lime and insulated with a layer of earth. Grass was sown on top of this to consolidate it and sheep were even employed to keep it trimmed! The exterior was designed by Durham architect Joseph Bonomi. Having spent time in Egypt studying the architecture there, he paradoxically adorned this futuristic mill with ancient Egyptian columns and motifs. The office block was copied from the Temple of Horus at Edfu on the Nile and the now demolished chimney resembled Cleopatra's needle.

Leeds Development Corporation plan to refurbish this area of industrial heritage as an acknowledgement of the contribution made by these flax spinners to the city's wealth.

Places of Interest in the Neighbourhood
36. What's in a Name? (Temple Newsam)
37. The World's Oldest Railway (Leeds)
39. The Sacrilegious Railway (Leeds)
40. Italian Towers and Moroccan Minarets (Leeds)
44. Cricket and Moravia (Fulneck)

39 The Sacrilegious Railway

Position: Leeds (W. Yorks)
O. S. Map: Leeds, Bradford & Harrogate Area Sheet: 104
Map Ref: SE306/334
Access: The church of St Peter is in Kirkgate, south-west of the city centre, between the railway and the river. The graveyard can be viewed from a tiny public park at the foot of the railway embankment.

The railway builders of the nineteenth-century were undoubtedly brilliant engineers but sometimes ruthless ones as well. This was especially so when obstacles stood in the way of the rapidly expanding rail network which spread across the country during this period. An example of this occurred in 1869 when a line came close to the centre of Leeds. The plan necessitated an embankment which didn't just pass close to the parish church of St Peter but which went straight through the graveyard itself. Accordingly the bodies were exhumed and reburied elsewhere and the railway was built. This episode would have been forgotten had not the headstones been set in rows across the embankment slopes like paving stones where they can still be seen today – when the grass is not too tall!

  The church is Victorian but replaced a medieval one, memorials from which, plus a fine Anglo-Saxon cross, can be seen inside.

Places of Interest in the Neighbourhood
36. What's in a Name? (Temple Newsam)
37. The World's Oldest Railway (Leeds)
38. The Egyptian Linen Mill (Leeds)
40. Italian Towers and Moroccan Minarets (Leeds)

40 Italian Towers and Moroccan Minarets

Position: Leeds (W. Yorks)
O. S. Map: Leeds, Bradford & Harrogate Area Sheet: 104
Map Ref: SE295/330; and see below
Access: The Tower Works are on Globe Road in the Holbeck area of
Leeds, west of the railway station; and see below for others.

Factory life in West Yorkshire mill towns was ultimately to depend on
the steam engine. This was attended to with care and pride, lovingly
polished and oiled and in the bigger factories housed in an architecturally ornate setting. Architects often looked abroad to such places as

Italianate factory chimneys in Holbeck, Leeds.

Italy or Morocco for exotic inspiration. The use of such models is typical of the Victorian neo-medieval idea of making industrial structures aesthetic.

A splendid example is the engine house at the Tower works in Holbeck in Leeds. Built in 1864 by Leeds architect Thomas Shaw to manufacture textile machinery, its chimney is a copy of the Lamberti bell tower (or "campanile") in Verona, Italy. In 1899 the installation of a dust extraction plant allowed local architect William Bakewell to design a second chimney based on Giotto's bell tower at Florence cathedral, complete with flagpole.

Meanwhile Samuel Cunliffe Lister's silk mill (SE156/338) on Heaton Road in the Manningham area of Bradford opened in 1870. It covered 28 acres, had a 350 yard long frontage and boasted 7,000 employees, making it the world's largest factory at the time. Dominating the skyline is its 240 feet high Italianate campanile chimney round the top of which its owner claimed a horse and carriage could be driven!

It was not only chimneys, however, which received the Mediterranean treatment. A fine example is the St Paul's House office block (SE295/338) in Park Square at the west end of the Headrow in Leeds city centre. It was originally built as a warehouse for Sir John Barran, pioneer of ready-made clothing. It is a heady concoction of Moorish brick and terracotta designed by Leeds architect Thomas Ambler. The original minarets and curved parapets along the roof have subsequently been replaced by fibreglass replicas!

Also worth seeing is the Florentine-Gothic Town Hall (SE164/329) on Market Street in the centre of Bradford. Opened in 1873 it is crowned by a 200 feet high tower modelled on that of the Palazzo Vecchio in Florence. It was built by the architects Lockwood and Manson.

Places of Interest in the Neighbourhood
36. What's in a Name? (Temple Newsam)
37. The World's Oldest Railway (Leeds)
38. The Egyptian Linen Mill (Leeds)
39. The Sacrilegious Railway (Leeds)
44. Cricket and Moravia (Fulneck)

41 Knock, Knock You're Saved!

Position: Adel (W. Yorks)
O. S. Map: Leeds, Bradford & Harrogate Area Sheet: 104
Map Ref: SE275/403
Access: Adel is a village on the north-west side of Leeds. Follow the A660 Otley Road and then the minor Eccup road north-east. The church is a mile along on the east side opposite open fields.

The church at Adel is one of the best and most complete Norman (twelfth century) churches in Yorkshire. Furthermore it can boast a curious bronze "sanctuary knocker" on the door of the south porch. Dated to the thirteenth century it takes the form of a monster's head, representing the gateway to Hell, disgorging a man's head. This is thought to symbolize the saving power of the church in delivering man from damnation. The gable of the porch shows Christ flanked by the symbols of the Evangelists and is sumptuously decorated with Norman carving. These themes are repeated on the chancel arch inside where the devil appears as a dragon drinking holy water one moment, and cowering the next as Christ is victorious over the devil.

Near the entrance to the churchyard can be seen some Norman sarcophagi with a special place carved out for the head. There are also some interesting old millstones from Adel Mill Farm and a stepped mounting block for horses just outside the gate.

Places of Interest in the Neighbourhood
38. The Egyptian Linen Mill (Leeds)
39. The Sacrilegious Railway (Leeds)
40. Italian Towers and Moroccan Minarets (Leeds)
42. Roadside Relics (Otley)

42 Roadside Relics

Position: Leeds-Otley road
O. S. Map: Leeds, Bradford & Harrogate Area Sheet: 104
Map Ref: See below
Access: The A660 runs from Leeds, 10 miles north-west to Otley.

Alongside many of today's roads can be seen relics which remind us of their historical development from ancient tracks with boundary posts and waymark stones, through monastic packhorse ways and turnpike coach roads, with their milestones and toll-houses, up to the present day. The road from Leeds city centre to the market town of Otley provides ample testimony for the more recent history of our roads (see No 49 for ancient tracks).

Starting from Leeds, on the right hand side just before the University is a small stepped stone from which to mount horses (SE291/353).

In Headingley, a mile on, in a wall next to the "Original Oak" inn, is a plaque (SE280/360) marking the site of an ancient wayside oak tree where the head of the Saxon local government (or "Wapentake") met with his top men. Leeds lay in the Wapentake of Skyrack (or Shireoak).

Half a mile further, on the left, can be seen an old metal trough

An old toll-house just outside Otley.

(SE276/367) for watering thirsty horses.

At intervals all along this stretch of the road can be seen sturdy mileposts (marked "MS" and "MP" on the map) listing up to half a dozen destinations and their distances. Also to be seen are the three-sided black and white Turnpike mileposts. The Turnpike Trust had been instigated in 1663 to maintain deteriorating tracks by charging the users. 1 ½ miles beyond Bramhope on a hairpin bend can be seen a former toll house (SE236/445) at the end of some cottages called Bar House Row. Here, a gate, or bar, would have prevented travellers using the road without paying a toll.

Shortly, Otley is reached, home not only of furniture maker Thomas Chippendale, whose statue can be seen, but also of "Harry Ramsden's", the world's largest fish and chip shop! The market square is dominated by the Butter Cross shelter and a memorial clock tower covered with commemorative plaques.

On the subject of milestones, a curious one, in the shape of an obelisk, stands on the side of the A65 Leeds-Ilkley road (SE253/364) near to the ruins of Kirkstall Abbey. It records the fact that it lies exactly 200 miles from both London and Edinburgh and commemorates the forge, established by the Abbey monks, which contributed to the growth of Leeds as an industrial city.

Places of Interest in the Neighbourhood
41. Knock, Knock You're Saved! (Adel)
43. The Tunnellers' Monument (Otley)
47. A Job for the Locals (Apperley Bridge)

43 The Tunnellers' Monument

Position: Otley (W. Yorks)
O. S. Map: Leeds, Bradford & Harrogate Area Sheet: 104
Map Ref: SE202/454
Access: Otley lies 10 miles north-west of Leeds. The monument is signposted up Church Lane, by the side of All Saints Church on Bondgate.

In the churchyard of All Saints is to be found a truly monumental memorial to the 23 navvies who lost their lives during the digging of the 2¼ mile long tunnel below Bramhope Moor on the Leeds-Thirsk railway. It was very dangerous work involving 2,300 men and 400 horses. The memorial takes the form of a 6 feet high scale model of the castellated northern entrance of the tunnel, with its polygonal turret and high round turret flanking the arch. The design is duplicated on the other side of the grave and both are connected by a short tunnel. It was erected with money subscribed by contractors, sub-contractors and survivors to the sum of £300, and is inscribed with quotations from the Bible.

The full-scale tunnel itself was built between 1845 and 1849 and was Britain's third longest. The larger turret was originally occupied by railway staff in charge of the tunnel but was later used as a store and is now derelict.

Places of Interest in the Neighbourhood
42. Roadside Relics (Otley)
47. A Job for the Locals (Apperley Bridge)

The tunnellers' monument in Otley.

44 Cricket and Moravia

Position: Fulneck (W. Yorks)
O. S. Map: Leeds, Bradford & Harrogate Area Sheet: 104
Map Ref: SE223/320
Access: Fulneck lies between Pudsey and Tong, 3 ½ miles east of
Bradford, and the Moravian settlement is signposted.

Len (later Sir Leonard) Hutton was born at No. 5 Fulneck on the 23rd
June 1916. One of England's greatest cricketers, his innings of 364 runs
at the Oval is legendary – so famous in fact that an old music hall
joke ran: – "Where's Leeds?", "Near Pudsey"! Len went to Littlemoor
Council School in Pudsey, then to Pudsey Grammar School for a year
to learn technical drawing. He joined Pudsey St Lawrence team in the
Bradford League. One of his great friends also lived in Fulneck, in
Woodlands Park Road. This was Herbert Sutcliffe, another very great
Yorkshire cricket captain.

  Sir Len remembered Fulneck as a "paradise", which oddly enough
was the name of one of the settlement buildings in a small Moravian
religious community which came to Fulneck in the 1730s, originally
from Bohemia. They were hardworking folk of simple faith who built a
fine settlement which can still boast the longest Georgian terrace in
Europe. They also built rows of terraces for men, women, married
couples and widows and a school for boys and one for girls. There is a
small Moravian folk museum, explaining the work of this immigrant
community, as well as a chapel, working pottery and a shop. How odd
to come to a little place like Fulneck – they obviously found it con-
genial.

Places of Interest in the Neighbourhood
38. The Egyptian Linen Mill (Leeds)
40. Italian Towers and Moroccan Minarets (Leeds)
45. Woollen Wonders (Bradford)
46. A Yorkshire Highgate (Bradford)
47. A Job for the Locals (Apperley Bridge)

The Chapel in the Moravian settlement at Fulneck.

45 Woollen Wonders

Position: Bradford (W. Yorks)
O. S. Map: Leeds, Bradford & Harrogate Area Sheet: 104
Map Ref: SE166/332 ("Little Germany"); and see below for others
Access: "Little Germany" lies on the hillside just east of the city centre
between the A647 Leeds Road and Church Bank next to Eastbrook
Well Roundabout; and see below for others.

The city of Bradford was once the centre of Yorkshire's world famous
woollen textile industry, of which several impressive remains can be
seen today.

"Little Germany" was the name given to the one-time centre of
Bradford's wool merchanting. The curious name reflects the fact that
many German merchants settled here in the 1820-30s. They quickly
established themselves as an influential group importing continental
wool, turning it into good cloth and exporting it back to Germany.
Between 1852 and 1874 they built 30 so-called "palace warehouses" for
the reception and bulk disposal of piece-goods, yarns and wool. Art-
istic inspiration was sought from Italy and the warehouses were endowed with elaborate frontages by leading local architects. Several
merchants patronised cultural institutions and philanthropic causes,
such as Charles Semon of Danzig who financed several hospitals and
became Bradford's first foreign mayor.

A little distance north-west of the city centre is the Conditioning
House (SE154/339), a unique structure in Britain. Built in 1902 it was
where an impartial assessment was made of the quality of locally
produced textiles.

Also of interest is the Wool Exchange in Market Street (SE164/332) in
the city centre, built in 1867 in a flamboyant Venetian-Flemish Gothic
style. On Market days on Mondays and Saturdays it was said "there
was not a single type of wool and hair for which a buyer could not be
found on the (ex)Change". At the Market Street entrance are statues
of Bishop Blaize, patron saint of wool combers, and Edward III,
who reversed the declining wool trade in the fourteenth century. The
elaborate interior with its high beamed roof and wrought iron decora-
tion reflected the wealth and pride of these nineteenth century textile
barons. There is also a statue of Richard Cobden, "The Apostle of Free
Trade", whose 1860 Commercial Treaty with France opened up the
huge continental market.

The full history of the textile industry is illustrated at the Industrial

The "Little Germany" warehouses in Bradford.

Museum on Moorside Road, 2 miles from the city centre off the A647 Harrogate Road, as well as at The British Wool Centre at Oak Mills, on Station Road in Clayton.

46 A Yorkshire Highgate

Position: Bradford (W. Yorks)
O. S. Map: Leeds, Bradford & Harrogate Area Sheet: 104
Map Ref: SE175/343
Access: Undercliffe cemetery is between Undercliffe Lane and the A658 Otley Road running north-east out of Bradford city centre.

Bradford's Undercliffe cemetery is situated dramatically on a hillside overlooking the mills where many of those interred made their living. It is a very Victorian place with its maze of avenues lined with row upon row of soot-blackened grave stones. They take every form – pinnacles, towers, obelisks, Celtic crosses, Classical temples, shrines, richly carved headstones and angels. Its variety makes it a fascinating area to wander round and it is Yorkshire's equivalent of London's Highgate cemetery.

The Bradford Cemetery Company brought the 26 acre site in 1851 and appointed William Gay, of Leicester cemetery, to design the layout and be the registrar.

The Undercliffe Lane entrance was once flanked by the Registrar's and Sexton's lodges. The east side of the cemetery is unconsecrated for Methodists and Baptists, whilst the larger west side is for Church of England burials and was consecrated in 1854 by the Bishop of Ripon. The cemetery was divided up into areas of varying quality depending on accessibility and view – the better the plot, the higher the price. Thus the wealthy were separated from the poor.

The central Boulevard is the impressive heart of the cemetery dominated by the flamboyant memorials of wealthy and influential mill-owners, wool barons and politicians. Typical is the Illingworth Mausoleum in ancient Egyptian style complete with Sphinxes. Daniel Illingworth founded the largest spinning business in Bradford and was later joined by his sons Alfred and Henry, who married daughters of businessman Sir Isaac Holden (see no. 56). The Mausoleum is in memory of Alfred (1827-1906) who was also a prominent politician, and the others are buried nearby.

Adjacent are two Gothic spires which are the Swithen Anderton and Atkinson Jowett memorials. The former, who died in 1860, was one of Bradford's most prominent wool barons as well as being a magistrate. The latter was an alderman, bank director and supporter of the Church of England, who died in 1886. A Graeco-Roman temple with carved angels stands nearby and commemorates Jonathan Holden (1828-1906), a relative of Sir Isaac. Meanwhile, a Baroque monument is

Flamboyant graves in Bradford's Undercliffe Cemetery.

in memory of the Behrens family, notably Sir Jacob (1806-1889), son of a Hamburg merchant, who made a fortune in the export trade.

The finest plot of all, overlooking the city, is occupied by a 30 feet high obelisk to Joseph Smith, a land surveyor.

It is no less interesting to view the graves of the ordinary folk including those killed in the wars from the Crimea onwards. In remoter areas of the cemetery the poor are buried several coffins deep.

Over 123,000 interments were made before the cemetery company ceased business in the mid 1970s.

Places of Interest in the Neighbourhood
44. Cricket and Moravia (Fulneck)
45. Woollen Wonders (Bradford)
47. A Job for the Locals (Apperley Bridge)
48. The Model Town of Sir Titus Salt (Saltaire)

47 A Job for the Locals

Position: Apperley Bridge (W. Yorks)
O. S. Map: Leeds, Bradford & Harrogate Area Sheet: 104
Map Ref: SE198/383
Access: Apperley Bridge lies 6 miles north-east of Bradford on the
A658. The tower is in the grounds of Woodhouse Grove School and is
visible from the road.

A folly tower to be found at Apperley Bridge was named after Robert
Elam who had bought Lower Wortley Manor in 1799. The hill on which
his tower now stands originally supported a pagoda put up by the
original owner but Elam demolished this. In its place he erected a tower,
completed in 1804, which gave much needed work to the unemployed of
the village. Locally, and probably without reason, it is called the Old
Water Tower.

Places of Interest in the Neighbourhood
44. Cricket and Moravia (Fulneck)
45. Woollen Wonders (Bradford)
46. A Yorkshire Highgate (Bradford)
48. The Model Town of Sir Titus Salt (Saltaire)
49. On Ancient Moorland Tracks (Bingley)

Elam's Tower at Apperley Bridge.

48 The Model Town of Sir Titus Salt

Position: Saltaire (W. Yorks)
O. S. Map: Leeds, Bradford & Harrogate Area Sheet: 104
Map Ref: SE140/381
Access: Saltaire is on the north side of the A657 Shipley-Bingley road.

Sir Titus Salt (1803-1876) was a rich and philanthropic Bradford industrialist who wanted to provide a workplace and housing for his workers in pleasant surroundings. To this end he abandoned his 4 textile mills in order to found a whole new and enormous mill in Saltaire around which he developed an entirely new model village.

It was he who introduced alpaca wool into England's textile industry. His new mill, which had at one time 2,500 workers, was based on a Venetian design with its chimney disguised as a campanile.

The model town consisted of 850 terraced houses. As well as being spacious (larger ones for senior staff), they were varied by having three-storeyed parts in the middle and end of the terrace. Saltaire was opened in 1871 and its population was then over 4,000. There were no gardens only backyards, but a very fine park was provided.

45 almshouses were built in Gothic style for those of "good moral character and incapacity for labour by reason of age, disease or infirmity". The hospital was also in the Gothic style. Other innovations and introductions were on-the-spot facilities for schooling, libraries, public baths, a Turkish bath and steam laundry. Sir Titus was a staunch Congregationalist and the fine church is a feature, but he did not allow alcohol to be consumed so there were no public houses.

Alpaca was eventually replaced by merino and the mill finally ceased production but the area is now being developed for leisure and shopping. Salt's boathouse is now a café.

Shipley Glen, beyond the river, is also worth a visit. It has a very curious tramway, cable-powered on a slope, which opened in 1895 and was closed in 1967 due to vandalism. It has now been renovated and covers a quarter of a mile journey through the picturesque woods up towards the moors.

Places of Interest in the Neighbourhood
46. A Yorkshire Highgate (Bradford)
47. A Job for the Locals (Apperley Bridge)
49. On Ancient Moorland Tracks (Bingley)
51. The Canal that goes Uphill (Bingley)

49 On Ancient Moorland Tracks

Position: Bingley (W. Yorks)
O. S. Map: Leeds, Bradford & Harrogate Area Sheet: 104
Map Ref: See below
Access: See below.

The ancient predecessors of our modern road network are all too easily
forgotten. Some, which offered gentle gradients, have been overlain and
hidden by tarmac. However, others, criss-crossing remote moorland
areas, clinging to hillsides and edges, are still walkable, offering a far
wilder prospect than today's motor routes. Such trackways are tangible
reminders of a bygone age when it was the by-ways and the hamlets
they connected which played a vital role in the economic and social life
of the country.

The presence of prehistoric Bronze Age and Roman remains littering
the bleak Ilkley, Baildon and Rombald moors north of Bingley (see no.
50) betray the ancient origins of some tracks. Others gained importance as packhorse ways developed during monastic times by the great
abbey estates. It was these which traversed the moors connecting the
Abbey granges with outlying hamlets and the great market towns such
as Otley. Packhorse trains, numbering from 20 to 40 beasts, carried
wool, coal, lead, peat and corn in their panniers. Also using this local network, and taking it well beyond the Pennines, were the drovers
roads, bringing sheep and cattle from Scotland, and the Salters' ways,
bringing salt from Cheshire.

Repeated usage often hollowed the tracks deep into the hills and some
were paved resulting in causeways (known locally as "causeys", see nos.
58 and 78). Detailed maps are needed to follow these roads, but an
easily accessible example can be found at Eldwick, near Bingley, on
Baildon Moor (SE134/410) where parts of a paved way extend from
Golcar Farm towards Birch Close Lane, helping connect Bingley with
Otley. A fine walled hollow way also lies to the west (SE122/410).

Streams were crossed by quaint, single-spanned packhorse bridges
with low parapets to protect the panniers, as at Beck Foot (SE103/385)
crossing Harden Beck south-west of Bingley.

After the dissolution of the monasteries these tracks continued in
heavy use in the seventeenth and eighteenth centuries, the Turnpike
Trust being set up in 1663 to exact tolls for their upkeep and im-
provement. Parliament also authorised the erection of guideposts (or
"stoops") at junctions. A couple of way markers can be seen at

An old packhorse way at Eldwick, near Bingley.

Abel Cross (103:SD986/307) on the old road from Heptonstall to Haworth. More curious is the waymarking stone in Calderdale at Withens Gate (103:SD970/231) on the summit of the route between Cragg and Mankinholes. Its Latin inscription reads "We praise thee, O Lord" and it is said that coffins were rested here on their journey to consecrated ground.

  Not until the Industrial Revolution, with its wheeled transport and valley-based towns, were new, flatter, more direct roads constructed (see no. 42).

Places of Interest in the Neighbourhood
48. The Model Town of Sir Titus Salt (Saltaire)
51. The Canal that goes Uphill (Bingley)
52. Halifax Houses (Riddlesden)
57. "Room at the Top" (Harden)

50 "On Ilkla Moor Baht 'At"

Position: Ilkley (W. Yorks)
O. S. Map: Leeds, Bradford & Harrogate Area Sheet: 104
Map Ref: SE115/473 (The Panorama Stone)
Access: Ilkley is in Wharfedale, 10 miles north-west of Bradford on the A65.

Apart from the song, the charming town of Ilkley in Wharfedale is famous for its surrounding moors. On them can be found spectacular natural rock formations like the Cow and Calf Rocks (SE130/468), as well as rocks bearing the curious prehistoric "cup-and-ring" carvings. The origins of these carvings are obscure but perhaps the stones mark the boundaries of sacred grounds. The Swastika Stone (SE097/469) on the hills overlooking the town is unique in Britain. It is late Bronze Age and the symbol may represent fire or alternatively eternity. It takes a steep climb up the moor to find it.

Fortunately another stone (the Panorama Stone, see above for map reference) decorated with ringed hollows and ladder patterns, has been rendered more accessible by being moved to the public garden opposite St Margaret's church on Queens Road which runs parallel to the High Street in the direction of the moors.

Another oddity here in Ilkley is All Saints Church which contains no less than 3 Anglo-Saxon crosses. One retains its original head and all three used to stand outside in the churchyard. Their carvings are among the north of England's finest Anglo-Saxon work and suggest that there may have been an Anglo-Saxon cemetery nearby.

Ilkley was a mineral spa in the eighteenth century but no longer, though Victorian plunge pools can still be seen at White Wells, at the top of Wells Road. Never mind, the fresh air is just as bracing, and people have walked the moor for many years, especially after the Bank Holidays Act of 1871, which sent swarms of mill-workers over from Airedale.

Places of Interest in the Neighbourhood
49. On Ancient Moorland Tracks (Bingley)
51. The Canal that goes Uphill (Bingley)
52. Halifax Houses (Riddlesden)

51 The Canal that goes Uphill

Position: Bingley (W. Yorks)
O. S. Map: Leeds, Bradford & Harrogate Area Sheet: 104
Map Ref: SE108/399
Access: Bingley is 5 miles north-west of Bradford on the A650 Keighley
road. The Five-Rise locks are signposted and are reached by a 1 ½ mile
canalside walk from the car-park.

The construction of a trans-Pennine canal, linking the east and west
coasts of the industrial north of England, was authorised in 1770 to
carry boats 60 feet long and 14 feet wide without off-loading. Finally
completed in 1816 and costing £824,000, it was 127 miles long, making
it the longest in Britain. However, there were considerable engineering
difficulties, one of which was the steep gradient at Bingley. The answer
was the spectacular Five-Rise locks of 1774, a steep staircase of five
inter-connected locks raising the canal 59 feet 2 inches over a distance
of 300 feet. A total of 91 locks, 2 tunnels and many aqueducts took the
canal to a height of 500 feet across the Pennines.

Places of Interest in the Neighbourhood
48. The Model Town of Sir Titus Salt (Saltaire)
49. On Ancient Moorland Tracks (Bingley)
52. Halifax Houses (Riddlesden)
53. How Yorkshire Mill Owners Lived (Keighley)
57. "Room at the Top" (Harden)

The Five-Rise locks on the canal at Bingley.

52 Halifax Houses

Position: Riddlesden (W. Yorks)
O. S. Map: Leeds, Bradford & Harrogate Area Sheet: 104
Map Ref: SE079/421
Access: Riddlesden is a mile north-east of Keighley on the A650, East Riddlesden Hall being signposted. It is a National Trust property open between April and October.

In and around Halifax during the seventeenth-century, wealthy clothiers were building their houses in a distinctive and showy Gothic style. These so-called "Halifax Houses" characteristically have long ranges of mullioned and transomed windows below battlemented gables topped with finials. The focal point was often an imposing porch sometimes with a rose window. The now blackened masonry is today sometimes highlighted with white pointing.

A fine example is at East Riddlesden where the old "Banqueting Hall" had been bought in 1638 by James Murgatroyd, a wealthy clothier from Warley. He set about ambitious extensions, including two porches with rose windows, finishing in 1648. The use of Classical columns on the porches is said to have been learned by Halifax masons sent to work on the Bodleian Library at Oxford. The Hall is furnished in period style and still retains its superb fireplace, oak panelling and decorative plaster ceilings.

In the grounds of the Hall is one of the finest Medieval timber-framed tithe barns in the north of England. It is 120 feet long and is considerably older than the Hall, and now houses a collection of farm implements. At the rear of the Hall is a walled Jacobean garden complete with monastic fishpond.

53 How Yorkshire Mill Owners Lived

Position: Keighley (W. Yorks)
O. S. Map: Leeds, Bradford & Harrogate Area Sheet: 104
Map Ref: SE055/422
Access: Cliffe Hall is on Spring Gardens Lane, half a mile north-west
out of Keighley town centre, off the A629 Skipton Road.

The Aire valley in which Keighley lies is a classic landscape in which to
explore the surviving relics of the Industrial Revolution in this part of
the old West Riding. The resulting community saw considerable dif-
ferences in standards of living, from the claustrophobic, soot-blackened
terraces of the factory workers in the valley bottoms, to the luxuriously
appointed mansions of the wealthy mill-owners set high up on the
wooded hillsides overlooking the workplace. Cliffe Hall is a noteworthy

A mill owner's castle at Keighley.

example of the latter, curious in that both exterior and interior remain much as they were a century ago. It was built in an Elizabethan style c.1830 by Christopher Netherwood, but sold in 1832 to local cotton mill owners, the Butterfield brothers. Between 1875 and 1880 the Hall was enlarged by Henry Isaac Butterfield and became Cliffe Castle, filled with works of art. Not until 1949 was it finally sold to Sir Bracewell Smith, a one-time MP and Lord Mayor of London. It was he who donated it to the Borough of Keighley thus enabling its conversion to a museum and art gallery. Most interesting is the suite of Victorian rooms furnished to resemble their original appearance complete with splendid glass chandeliers. The other rooms include a display of local industrial history as well as a model of a clog-making shop from nearby Silsden.

Places of Interest in the Neighbourhood
51. The Canal that goes Uphill (Bingley)
52. Halifax Houses (Riddlesden)
54. Shrine to the Brontës (Haworth)
55. Grave Situations (Haworth)
56. A Hidden Folly Garden (Oakworth)

The Brontë Parsonage at Haworth.

54 Shrine to the Brontës

Position: Haworth (W. Yorks)
O. S. Map: Leeds, Bradford & Harrogate Area Sheet: 104
Map Ref: SE029/372
Access: Haworth is 3 ½ miles south-west of Keighley on the A6033 and
the Brontë Parsonage Museum is in Church Street.

Haworth, a small picturesque hill town, was the setting for the remarkable literary flowering of the Brontë family and as a result is visited by
hundreds of literary devotees and academics every year. The writers
were the daughters of the Rev. Patrick Brontë, of Cornish-Irish descent,
who settled in the area in 1820. Their story is one of literary genius
overcoming hardship. They lived short lives, Anne reaching 29 years,
Emily 30, and Charlotte 38. Their mother died only a year after they
came to St Michael's in Haworth but their father survived them all to
live to be 84. Their brother Bramwell died at 31, his talent as a painter
wasted by drink and opium. The public house which he frequented, the
Black Bull, is still there.

The sisters were born in Thornton, near Bradford, where there is a
plaque on their birthplace, but they are all buried in the family vault at
Haworth except for Anne, who lies in Scarborough. As for the church,
it was rebuilt after the Brontës had died and only the tower is original,
on which it is said can be seen the marks of bullets. The Rev. Brontë
used apparently to fire his pistol out of his bedroom window! Only
Charlotte married, her father's curate in 1854, but she died the following year.

Their first published work, a joint collection called *Poems by Currer,
Ellis and Acton Bell* was not a publishing success but Charlotte's novel
Jane Eyre was spectacularly so in 1847. Emily's *Wuthering Heights* and
Anne's *Agnes Grey* were published in the same year but the former only
achieved its huge fame posthumously. The grandeur, harsh at times, of
the local scenery shaped their novels and the climate, bleak at times,
helped produce the illnesses which carried them off so early.

Places of Interest in the Neighbourhood
52. Halifax Houses (Riddlesden)
53. How Yorkshire Mill Owners Lived (Keighley)
55. Grave Situations (Haworth)
56. A Hidden Folly Garden (Oakworth)
57. "Room at the Top" (Harden)

55 Grave Situations

Position: Haworth (W. Yorks); and see below for others
O. S. Map: Leeds, Bradford & Harrogate area; and see below for others
Sheet:104; and see below for others
Map Ref: SE023/371; and see below for others
Access: Haworth is 3½ miles south-west of Keighley on the A6033 and
St Michael's churchyard lies out of the town past the vicarage and
across the moor. The grave of Lily Cove is on the right-hand-side upon
entry; and see below for others.

South and west Yorkshire has its fair share of graves with curious tales
attached, but space permits only a selection to be given here.

In St Michael's churchyard at Haworth is the grave of professional
balloonist and parachutist Lily Cove (see above for access). On June
11th, 1906 at the age of 21 she made a balloon ascent at Haworth gala
from which she made a parachute descent. Unfortunately she became
detached and fell to her death. Other graves of those whose lives were
cut dramatically short include Robert Gully in St. Cuthbert's at Ackworth (111: SE440/181) east of Wakefield, murdered by Chinese after
being shipwrecked off Formosa in 1842; 19 year-old Robert Millthorp
killed by a falling gravestone in front of All Saints' church at Darfield
(111: SE419/044) near Barnsley; a charcoal burner whose hut burned
down deep in Ecclesall Woods in south-east Sheffield (111: SK325/825);
the 10-man crew of a World War II bomber damaged in 1944 over
Germany which crashed in Endcliffe Park on Ecclesall Road in Sheffield
(111: SK328/858); and the 402 people who died during Sheffield's 1832
cholera epidemic and are buried around a monument in Norfolk Park
in the city centre (111: SK362/866).

Rather more deserving of his fate was David Hartley, whose
headstone lies in front of the porch of the old St Thomas' church in
Heptonstall (103: SD986/280) near Hebden Bridge. He was one of the
notorious Cragg Vale Coiners hung at York for clipping gold off
sovereigns.

Some graves leave no doubt as to the former professions and inter-
ests of those interred, as in the case of the chimney-shaped grave in
Beckett Street cemetery in Leeds (104: SE318/346) to England's oldest
steeplejack; the beer barrel shaped grave in St John's at Kirkheaton
(110: SE180/183) east of Huddersfield to a local drinker; the tomb of
Benjamin Coldwell in St George's churchyard in Portobello Street in
Sheffield city centre (111: SK354/875) on which is carved the music of

his favourite hymn; and a blacksmith's grave in the centre of Barnsley cemetery (111: SE355/055) on Cemetery Road, on which are carved all the tools of his trade.

Curious and interesting achievements are recorded on graves such as Sexton Hezekiah Briggs buried at All Saints in Bingley, north-west of Bradford, who interred over 7,000 corpses; Dr. Nicholas Saunderson buried at St. John the Baptist's in Penistone (110: SE246/034) west of Barnsley who, despite being born blind, went on to become a Cambridge mathematics professor; Alexander John Scott buried at St. Mary's in Ecclesfield (110: SK353/942) north of Sheffield who was chaplain to Lord Nelson at Trafalgar; and Enoch Taylor the machine maker buried at St. Bartholomews in Marsden (110: SE048/117) south-west of Huddersfield, whose Christian name was given by the Luddites to the great hammers they used to destroy his work, "Enoch did make them and Enoch shall smash them".

The oldest people to have been buried include a man interred in 1635 at St. Peter's in Thorner (104: SE380/405) north-east of Leeds who was 117 and Hannah Scott who was buried in Dewsbury west of Wakefield at the dubious age of 814!

Barnburgh (111: SE484/033) to the west of Doncaster was once known as the "cat and man town". The man was the knight Percival Cresacre and the cat was a wild one which attacked and killed him in the porch of St. Peter's church. A sculpture of the cat sits at the foot of his fourteenth-century tomb. Another knight, Roger Rockley, is buried inside St. Mary's at Worsborough (111: SE350/026), south of Barnsley. The tomb is remarkable in that it takes the form of an oak bunk bed – on top is the knight in armour but below is the same man after death represented as a frightening, grinning skeleton.

For other graves see nos. 25,43,46 and 68.

56 A Hidden Folly Garden

Position: Oakworth (W. Yorks)
O. S. Map: Leeds, Bradford & Harrogate Area Sheet: 104
Map Ref: SE034/389
Access: Oakworth lies in the Worth Valley 2½ miles south-west of
Keighley on the B6143 and the Municipal Park is on Colne Road.

Oakworth Municipal Park was once the site of Oakworth House, home
of Sir Isaac Holden (1807-97) inventor and prosperous textile manufac-
turer who owned factories in Bradford and France. He ate mainly fruit
and to keep him supplied he built forty hot houses in the grounds. To
heat them he used fourteen boilers, 37,000 feet of piping and three
purpose-built reservoirs!

Of his Italianate mansion only the entrance porch remains but some-
thing of his eccentric folly garden remains today. His greatest feat was
the construction of a Winter garden with Turkish bath at the rear of the
house for his wife in inclement weather. It is suggested that he spent
anything between £30,00 and £120,000 on this project alone. Water was
fed directly into a pool from the moors above and the whole was roofed
with coloured glass supported on cast iron trusses.

Between 1864 and 1874 French and Italian workers laboured hard to
convert the grounds into a subterranean world of caves and grottoes.
Although the Winter garden no longer survives, the visitor can still see
the grottoes, Summer House, cascade, sham rusticated masonry walls
and mock fossilised trees which conceal staircases up to the hanging
gardens on an upper level.

Nearby runs the Keighley and Worth Valley steam railway which was
used as a setting for the popular period film "The Railway Children".
Opened in 1867 it boasts splendid Victorian stations at Oakworth,
Haworth, Ingrow and Damems.

Places of Interest in the Neighbourhood
52. Halifax Houses (Riddlesden)
53. How Yorkshire Mill Owners Lived (Keighley)
54. Shrine to the Brontës (Haworth)
55. Grave Situations (Haworth)
57. "Room at the Top" (Harden)

The remains of Sir Isaac Holden's house at Oakworth.

57 "Room at the Top"

Position: Harden (W. Yorks)
O. S. Map: Leeds, Bradford & Harrogate Area Sheet: 104
Map Ref: SE095/378
Access: Harden is a village 2 ½ miles west of Bingley on the B6429. St. David's Ruin is best reached from the Malt Shovel pub which is on the bridge over Harden Beck. Walk up the hill away from the village turning left up a steep track to open fields at the top. Turn left through a gate just before an isolated barn and walk over to the woods turning left along a track following the ridge.

St. David's Ruin, although it differs from his description, provided inspiration for Bradford-born John Braine's fictional Gothic St. Clair Folly, in which a scene from his novel *Room at the Top* occurs. The ruin itself is in fact a folly castle built in 1796 by Benjamin Ferrand as an eyecatcher for Harden Grange, the family home, across the Harden Valley below towards Bingley. His initials and date are carved in the pointed door arch. The ruin was tidied up in the 1950s when the romantically ruined tower, which comprised a window surrounded by intentionally crumbling masonry, was truncated into a neat cylinder with a ledge marking the start of the second storey. A piece of ruined wall with a pointed arch stands nearby but was probably once connected. This tower-and-arch folly is one of the finest examples of this type of ruin in the country.

Half a mile to the north of Harden Grange, over the B6429, is St. Ives, the house where the nineteenth-century Ferrand family lived. Here, W. B. Ferrand created a grand romantic landscape. A track to the north leads to a steep crag called the "Druid's Altar" (SE093/400), a scene which so excited Disraeli that he included it in his book *Sybil* as the background to a Chartist meeting. To the south-east is the Fairfax Intrenchment (SE085/394), a long earthwork said to have been a Civil War defence and incorporated into an area set out as a wild heather park. A boulder with inscribed tablet is nearby marking the spot where Ferrand's mother-in-law, Lady Blantyre, used to sit, as well as an obelisk to Ferrand himself listing his achievements.

Places of Interest in the Neighbourhood
51. The Canal that goes Uphill (Bingley)
52. Halifax Houses (Riddlesden)
53. How Yorkshire Mill Owners Lived (Keighley)

St David's Ruin in the woods above Harden.

58 The Department of Curious Names

Position: Egypt (W. Yorks)
O. S. Map: Leeds, Bradford & Harrogate Area Sheet: 104
Map Ref: SE091/338
Access: Egypt is a hamlet a mile north of Thornton on the B6145, 4½ miles west of Bradford.

Egypt is in West Yorkshire! It is the local name for what was originally a quarryman's settlement established for the extraction of the fine local gritstone. Its name reflects the fact that quarrying began about the time of the Napoleonic Wars when Napoleon went into Egypt and also to Moscow. According to Kendal and Wroot's *Geology of Yorkshire*, the fact that a small outflank in the neighbourhood is known locally as Moscow similarly reflects local interest in European events.

The road through Egypt ran down the valley through a man-made gorge composed of massive gritstone blocks, 30-40 feet high and up to 15-20 feet in thickness. These walls retained thousands of tons of quarry waste and were erected by the local workers. The whole structure was known as "The Walls of Jericho", perhaps because it would resist the sound of many trumpets. The stone quarried here was used for flagstones in the nearby villages of Denholme, Thornton and Allerton, as well as for a fine pack-horse causeway running to Atherton.

Unfortunately the walls were demolished in the mid 1980s and little remains to be seen today other than a wall next to the houses in the valley bottom.

Other curious names which may or may not have similarly odd derivations include, in West Yorkshire ,Goose Eye, Scapegoat Hill, Catherine Slack, Triangle, California, Canada and Hades, whilst in south Yorkshire can be found Wales, Paris and Rhodesia!

Places of Interest in the Neighbourhood
48. The Model Town of Sir Titus Salt (Saltaire)
51. The Canal that goes Uphill (Bingley)
54. Shrine to the Brontës (Haworth)
56. A Hidden Folly Garden (Oakworth)
57. "Room at the Top" (Harden)

59 From Weavers to Clog Makers

Position: Heptonstall and Hebden Bridge (W. Yorks)
O. S. Map: Blackburn, Burnley & surrounding Area Sheet: 103
Map Ref: SD986/280 (Heptonstall) and SD992/272 (Hebden Bridge)
Access: Hebden Bridge is about 9 miles north-west of Halifax on the
A646 Burnley Road, and Heptonstall is approached by a minor road
from there.

The hill-top village of Heptonstall is reached up a steep cobbled packhorse way called "The Buttress", from Hebden Bridge in the valley
below. It has many sturdily built sandstone weavers' cottages with their
characteristic weavers' windows, as many as 9 to a row, divided by
stone mullions.

Heptonstall is also noteworthy for its two churches (one ruined) in
one churchyard which also contains the grave of the famous American
poet Sylvia Plath (1932-1963) as well as that of David Hartley, the
infamous "clipper" of gold coins (see no. 55). The "Octagon" nearby is
probably the oldest Methodist chapel in continuous use in the world.
Built in the late eighteenth-century its roof was custom built in Rotherham and delivered by horse and cart.

The reason why the houses in Hebden Bridge are of more recent construction is mechanisation. In the eighteenth-century hand looms were
replaced by water-powered spinning machines built along the rivers in
the valley bottom. However, space was at a premium and so "top-to-
bottom" terraces were built. These were laid out along the steep valley
sides and were divided down the axis of the terrace rather than through
its thickness. Thus, the houses along one side opened on a different level
to those further down the slope on the other. The larger house at the
end of each row was for the foreman.

Hebden Bridge is also known for Walkley's Clog Mill, probably the
most famous clog factory in Britain. There is also a fine Victorian station, a Tudor bridge, and an Austin Morris motor museum. Finally
there is Mitclough Mill which was founded in 1870 and was the first
co-operative. It was run on a profit-sharing basis as the Hebden Bridge
Manufacturing Co-operative Society.

Places of Interest in the Neighbourhood
60. Once England's Biggest Sub-Post Office (Todmorden)
61. The Monument with Political Leanings (Todmorden)

60 Once England's Biggest Sub-Post Office

Position: Todmorden (W. Yorks)
O. S. Map: Blackburn, Burnley & surrounding Area Sheet: 103
Map Ref: SD935/241
Access: Todmorden is 10 miles west of Halifax on the A646 and the Old
Hall is on Hall Street in the town centre, close to the railway station.

It is perhaps appropriate in England's largest county that we should
find what was reckoned to be the biggest sub-post office in the country.
This was not quite true as the post office actually occupied only a small
part of a much larger and grander building. This is Todmorden Old
Hall, a fine house with a gabled frontage and mullioned windows.
Inside its panelled hall can be seen a fireplace dated 1603. Recently,
however, the building has been converted into a restaurant although a
post box is still on the pavement outside.

Nearby is the Town Hall (SD938/242), a similarly grand structure but
this time resembling a Classical Greek temple. It is topped with a group
of figures surrounding a plinth on which is inscribed "Yorkshire and
Lancashire", for the building lies astride what was once the county
boundary.

Places of Interest in the Neighbourhood
59. From Weavers to Clog Makers (Heptonstall – Hebden Bridge)
61. The Monument with Political Leanings (Todmorden)
66. The Road with Mysterious Origins (Littleborough)

Stoodley Pike obelisk overlooking Todmorden.

61 The Monument with Political Leanings

Position: Todmorden
O. S. Map: Blackburn, Burnley & surrounding Area Sheet: 103
Map Ref: SD974/242
Access: The monument is situated on the Pennine Way overlooking Todmorden, 2 miles to the west. It is reached via the hamlets of Lumbutts and Mankinholes off the A6033 Todmorden – Rochdale road, 2 miles south of Todmorden.

The colossal 120 feet high obelisk of Stoodley Pike has a somewhat chequered, not to mention ominous, architectural history. It was first commissioned by local gentry in 1814 as a peace monument to commemorate the surrender of Paris, and was to be financed by public subscription. However, construction was halted when it was heard that Napoleon had escaped from Elba. The obelisk was not completed until victory was sealed at Waterloo in 1815.

The chunky column with its conical top looked set to stand forever but toppled on February 8th, 1854, the very day the Russian Ambassador left London prior to the start of the Crimean War. A successor was planned with the same height but of a different design. Designed by local architect James Green it was finished in time to commemorate the British-Russian peace and it was strengthened by 8 buttresses.

From then on Stoodley Pike obelisk seems to have lost all interest in political events and has required little attention beyond being given a lightning conductor in 1889!

Places of Interest in the Neighbourhood
59. From Weavers to Clog Makers (Heptonstall – Hebden Bridge)
60. Once England's Biggest Sub-Post Office (Todmorden)
66. The Road with Mysterious Origins (Littleborough)

62 Wainhouse's Folly Chimney

Position: Halifax (W. Yorks)
O. S. Map: Leeds, Bradford & Harrogate Area Sheet: 104
Map Ref: SE078/240
Access: The chimney is reached from the A646 south-west of Halifax town centre.

Wainhouse's Tower, Column or Folly, dating from around 1871, is probably the strangest structure in West Yorkshire (see frontispiece). Standing 275 feet high on a hill overlooking Halifax, it was originally designed as a chimney to carry away the smoke from J. E. Wainhouse's Washer Lane Dyeworks by means of a connecting flue. This was necessary due to the Smoke Abatement Act of 1870. The first concept was of a brick chimney surrounded by a spiral staircase and outside that a stone casing. It was unfinished when Wainhouse, a wealthy man, sold the works to his manager who was unable to finish the chimney. Wainhouse then had it completed by another architect as a combined belvedere and look-out tower but, like every building he was connected with in and around Halifax from the humblest terrace (e. g. Wainhouse Terrace) upwards, he insisted on it being decorated. Not just decorated in this case, but positively covered with Gothic ornament. It was topped by a lantern-like structure which made its possible use as an observatory practically impossible due to the lack of space for a telescope!

After Wainhouse's death the bottom 6 feet of the tower were used as a henhouse! Then in World War II it was occasionally used by the military as an observation tower. It belongs to Calderdale Borough and is open on certain days, but remember that a 400 step staircase awaits you!

Places of Interest in the Neighbourhood
63. Alms for "Old Tristram" (Halifax)
64. Heads you Lose! (Halifax)
65. "Pieces of Cloth" (Halifax)

(For illustration see Frontispiece)

63 Alms for "Old Tristram"

Position: Halifax
O. S. Map: Leeds, Bradford & Harrogate Area Sheet: 104
Map Ref: SE097/253
Access: Halifax is 7 miles south-west of Bradford and St. John's church
is near the railway station on King Street.

Alms-boxes, or poor boxes, used to be a feature of many churches.
They enabled charitable people to subscribe to the welfare of the parish
poor. One of the most unusual is in St. John's church in Halifax, itself
one of the largest parish churches in England.

"Old Tristram" in St John's church at Halifax.

It takes the form of a life-sized carved and painted wooden figure of a man holding out a collection box. It is believed to date back to 1701 but may be seventeenth-century due to the figure's garb. Known as "Old Tristram", the original name may have been Trosteram after an old family of Halifax shoemakers, or else he may have been just a beggar who stood in the church porch collecting for the parish poor. On his death his effigy was carved and he still collects for the poor of Halifax with his carved scroll on his chest asking "Pray Remember the Poor". Such alms-boxes are decidedly rare.

Places of Interest in the Neighbourhood
62. Wainhouse's Folly Chimney (Halifax)
64. Heads you Lose! (Halifax)
65. "Pieces of Cloth" (Halifax)

64 Heads you Lose!

Position: Halifax (W. Yorks)
O. S. Map: Leeds, Bradford & Harrogate Area Sheet: 104
Map Ref: SE090/252
Access: Halifax is 7 miles south-west of Bradford and the gibbet can be found on Gibbet Street running west out of the town centre.

In Gibbet Street there still stands a gibbet, albeit a replica of the original. The Halifax gibbet (hence the early Yorkshire prayer, "From Hell, Hull and Halifax, Good Lord Deliver Us") was not a gallows but

A replica of the notorious Halifax guillotine.

a form of guillotine, invented long before the one used in the French Revolution. Although the site is now surrounded by buildings it was once a hill outside the town. The blade fell on the release of a rope by the bailiff. If an animal had been stolen, the animal itself pulled the rope releasing the blade!

If a thief stole a piece of cloth worth more than 13 pence he was sentenced to be beheaded. If he was very agile and escaped from under the blade and ran across the river he was pardoned, according to one authority. However, according to another, the only man known to have escaped by crossing the town boundary, John Lacy, returned to Halifax later and was executed in 1623. The public house "The Running Man" celebrates his temporary reprieve. For the morbid or curious the original blade may be seen in the Calderdale Industrial Museum in the Piece Hall, weighing nearly 6 pounds and measuring almost a foot in length.

Some form of gibbet is recorded as early as Norman times, along with other places, but the Halifax gibbet lasted longer than all of them, in fact until 30 April, 1650. It is recorded that 52 people were executed from 1541-1650 making 80 in total.

Places of Interest in the Neighbourhood
62. Wainhouse's Folly Chimney (Halifax)
63. Alms for "Old Tristram" (Halifax)
65. "Pieces of Cloth" (Halifax)

65 "Pieces of Cloth"

Position: Halifax (W. Yorks)
O. S. Map: Leeds, Bradford & Harrogate Area Sheet: 104
Map Ref: SE095/251
Access: Halifax is 7 miles south-west of Bradford. The Piece Hall is on Horton Street in the town centre.

The "Piece Hall" is the exchange where wool merchants came to see and buy "pieces" of cloth from weavers working in the cottage industries in the surrounding area. It comprises 315 small rooms off colonnaded galleries around a central cobbled quadrangle and has two or three storeys. It is similar to an Italian piazza.

Market stalls in the Halifax Piece Hall.

It is the only cloth hall to survive in Yorkshire and the building dates from 1778. The main gate is in Westgate and has a cupola, a bell to sound opening and closing of business hours and a golden fleece on the weather-vane. With the coming of factories, the need for the Piece Hall dwindled as more direct deals could now be made so in 1871 it was converted for the next century into a wholesale fruit and vegetable market.

In the 1970s it was restored and is now used as combined local government offices together with craft and antique shops, a café, and an art galley. There is an open market on Saturday and also direct access to the Calderdale Industrial Museum with its steam engines and looms.

Places of Interest in the Neighbourhood
62. Wainhouse's Folly Chimney (Halifax)
63. Alms for "Old Tristram" (Halifax)
64. Heads you Lose! (Halifax)

The mysterious paved road over Blackstone Edge near Littleborough.

66 The Road with Mysterious Origins

Position: Littleborough (W. Yorks)
O. S. Map: Manchester and surrounding areas Sheet:109
Map Ref: SE974/172
Access: Littleborough is 11 miles south-west of Halifax on the A58. The Roman Road is best reached from the White House Inn following the Pennine Way south, on the other side of the road, for about two thirds of a mile.

A curious paved road runs along Blackstone Edge over the crest of a steep hill on the Yorkshire-Greater Manchester border. Its sturdily constructed and cambered surface of large cobbles is 18 feet wide with even larger, troughed stones, down the middle. The origin of this carefully built road is a cause for controversy. Many scholars believe it was the work of the Romans in order to connect Manchester (Mancunium) to Ilkley (Olicana) across the bleak Pennine moors inhabited by the Brigante tribe. Documentary evidence for this lies in the many Roman coins found in the area depicting, amongst others, the Emperor Hadrian. On the other hand, it has been claimed that the road is Medieval and was part of the pack-horse way down the Ryburn Valley.

Either way, this exposed hill road with its splendid views was an important South Pennine crossing and was used by Daniel Defoe in 1705. His diary records how he got lost in a blizzard – in August! The road was replaced by a turnpike road in 1735 which opted for an easier gradient, and again in 1786 by an even less steep route which became the Rochdale-Lancashire road.

Places of Interest in the Neighbourhood
59. From Weavers to Clog Makers (Heptonstall – Hebden Bridge)
60. Once England's Biggest Sub-Post Office (Todmorden)
61. The Monument with Political Leanings (Todmorden)
67. England's Longest Canal Tunnel (Marsden)

67 England's Longest Canal Tunnel

Position: Marsden (W. Yorks)
O. S. Map: Sheffield & Huddersfield Area Sheet: 110
Map Ref: SE040/120
Access: Marsden is 8 ½ miles south-west of Huddersfield and the canal entrance is beyond the town at Tunnel End.

There are two Huddersfield canals. Huddersfield Narrow canal is almost 20 miles long from Huddersfield to Ashton-Under Lyne, and was finished in 1811. It was closed to traffic in 1944 though a boat did get through in 1948. Many locks had their gates removed and concrete ramps fitted so the plans of the Huddersfield Canal Society to eventually restore navigation are indeed ambitious and costly. One of its most spectacular features is Standedge Tunnel which pierces Standedge Fell in the Pennines (Standedge is a nineteenth-century corruption of the more accurate Stanedge or stone-edge). It is the longest canal tunnel in the country at 3 miles 176 yards (5 kilometres) and accounted for much of the £400,000 bill which the canal incurred. A rail tunnel runs alongside it, its exhaust shafts coming out on the moors above.

The rail tunnel was built by the Huddersfield and Manchester railway company who bought the canal in 1844. Although canal receipts were flagging, ownership of the canal tunnel reduced construction costs of the rail tunnel by some £70,000 since it facilitated quick earth removal and more accurate tunnelling estimates.

Huddersfield's other canal is the Huddersfield Broad Canal which is 3¾ miles long and is now navigable by motor cruisers. It is distinguished by stone-built bridges close to the locks and more especially by the extraordinary Turnbridge near Aspley Basin which, by a Heath Robinson-looking system of girders, wheels and chains, lifts the deck of the bridge vertically parallel to the water.

Places of Interest in the Neighbourhood
66. The Road with Mysterious Origins (Littleborough)

The entrance to the Standedge canal tunnel at Marsden.

68 Robin Hood's Grave

Position: Brighouse (W. Yorks)
O. S. Map: Leeds, Bradford & Harrogate Area Sheet: 104
Map Ref: SE174/215
Access: The grave lies in Kirklees Park on the A644 Wakefield road
running south-east out of Brighouse, through Clifton, below the M62
and through Kirklees. It is on private property and permission must be
sought from the Estate Office, Kirklees Estate, Mirfield, Yorkshire.

Many scholars believe an outlaw existed in England during the eleventh
and twelfth centuries but there is little tangible evidence to link him
with the Brighouse area. However, a local legend runs that an ageing
Robin Hood became ill and sought help from his "kinswoman" the
Prioress Elizabeth de Stayton at Kirklees Priory. Unfortunately his
trust was ill-founded as the Prioress was a great friend of Sir Roger de
Doncaster, an arch enemy of Robin's. Ostensibly curing him by drain-
ing off some bad blood, the Prioress bled Robin to death in the upper
room of the gate-house, which still stands. Shortly before dying he
summoned his lieutenant, Little John, to bring him his bow. He shot his
last arrow some 600 yards and asked to be buried where it landed – in
Kirklees Park. The stone covering the grave was believed by locals to
have magic curative powers and pieces were chipped off as amulets.
Navvies working on the Yorkshire and Lancashire railway even put
pieces under their pillows to cure toothache! Eventually a wall topped
with railings was erected around the grave. In the wall is a stone
inscribed with a seventeenth-century mock-Medieval inscription which
translates thus:

> Here underneath this little stone
> Lies Robert Earl of Huntingdon
> Never was there an archer so good
> And people called him Robin Hood
> Such outlaws as he and his men
> Will England never see again
> December 1247

Places of Interest in the Neighbourhood
69. Two Churchless Steeples (Mirfield)
70. Cheap and Shoddy (Batley)
72. A Couple of Curious Clock Towers (Huddersfield)
73. "The Most Splendid Station Facade in England" (Huddersfield)
74. Four Thousand Years of History (Almondbury)

69 Two Churchless Steeples

Position: Mirfield (W. Yorks)
O. S. Map: Leeds, Bradford & Harrogate Area Sheet: 104
Map Ref: SE178/212
Access: The Dumb or Doom Steeple is on the roundabout at the junction of the A644 Brighouse road and the A62 Huddersfield-Leeds road.

The so-called "Dumb Steeple" looks like a pinnacle from a demolished church but was never in fact part of a building. It is thought to have been a "doom steeple" which offered sanctuary to those fearful of judgement. It was also used as a midnight rendezvous at the beginning of the nineteenth century by the Luddites, those opposed to the introduction of new and efficient mechanical devices in the textile industry.

Mirfield's "Doom Steeple".

Mirfield's other churchless steeple was once part of St. Mary's church (SE212/205) which is reached east through Mirfield along Dunbottle Lane off the A62. This thirteenth-century church, with the exception of the tower, was rebuilt in 1825 but less than 50 years later was demolished again to make way for the present parish church. The tower still remains, isolated in the churchyard, as well as a round pier built into the new vestry.

Places of Interest in the Neighbourhood
68. Robin Hood's Grave (Brighouse)
70. Cheap and Shoddy (Batley)
72. A Couple of Curious Clock Towers (Huddersfield)
73. "The Most Splendid Station Facade in England" (Huddersfield)
74. Four Thousand Years of History (Almondbury)

The so-called Shoddy Temple in Batley.

70 Cheap and Shoddy

Position: Batley (W. Yorks)
O. S. Map: Leeds, Bradford & Harrogate Area Sheet: 104
Map Ref: SE237/247
Access: Batley is 8 miles south-west of Leeds on the A62 and the chapel
is on Commercial Street on one side of the central square along with the
police station and library.

The word "shoddy" has acquired a pejorative sense since the times
when it meant a cloth manufactured from old rags mixed with new wool
to make a reasonably-priced cloth. A fortune was made by the so-called
"Shoddy King", Benjamin Law of Gomersal, who is buried at Batley.
The process was widely practiced in Batley and Dewsbury.

The nickname of the "Shoddy Temple" was applied to the Central
Chapel in the square in Batley which dates from 1869. Many "Shoddy"
deals were done on its steps after Sunday service.

These rag merchants tried hard to compensate for the poor image of
their business by investing in fine buildings as witnessed by the imposing warehouses near the railway station (SE250/237). These have a
curved crescent-like facade and cusped Moorish arches.

The full history of "shoddy" is illustrated in the Dewsbury Museum at
Crows Nest Park on Heckmondwike Road.

Places of Interest in the Neighbourhood
44. Cricket and Moravia (Fulneck)
68. Robin Hood's Grave (Brighouse)
69. Two Churchless Steeples (Mirfield)

71 The Bridge Chapel of St. Mary's

Position: Wakefield (W. Yorks)
O. S. Map: Leeds, Bradford & Harrogate Area Sheet: 104
Map Ref: SE338/202
Access: The chapel lies on the outskirts of the town on the A61 south to
Barnsley.

There are only 4 chantry or bridge chapels surviving in England and 2
are in the area covered by this book (the other is a fine example in
Rotherham, see no. 9). Their purpose was to act as toll-houses to collect
alms from religious pilgrims for the upkeep of the bridge, as well as for
purposes of defence, and as structural reinforcement for the bridge.

This one was endowed by Edmund, Duke of York, in 1398 and erected
half a century earlier. It has had two restorations, one by Sir George
Gilbert Scott in 1847 and another more recently in the late 1930s.
During the 1847 work the original spectacular but crumbling west front
was transferred to Kettlethorpe Hall three miles away (see no. 27). The
chapel itself comprises seven windows and a small crypt. The latter is in
a cellar reached by a spiral staircase in the corner turret.

It has considerable and curious charm and a chequered history beginning in 1342 when it acted as a toll bridge and for religious uses. Then in
the sixteenth-century it was used by plague victims to prevent the
spread of infection to users of the nearby Parish church, now the
cathedral. Then about 1780 it was an old clothes shop, in 1829 a
newsroom, and in 1842 it was transferred to the Commissioners of the
Church of England.

Places of Interest in the Neighbourhood
27. The Moving Bridge Chapel (Newmillerdam)
28. An Eccentric but Enlightened Squire (Walton)
29. Keeping Cool at Nostell Priory (Wragby)

72 A Couple of Curious Clock Towers

Position: Huddersfield (W. Yorks)
O. S. Map: Sheffield & Huddersfield Area Sheet: 110
Map Ref: SE163/165
Access: Ravensknowle Park clock tower is in Ravensknowle Park, 1 ½ miles east of Huddersfield centre on the Wakefield road.

The first clock tower is to be found in Ravensknowle Park which was itself donated to Huddersfield as a first World War memorial. After the Huddersfield Cloth Hall (1798) was demolished in 1929, parts were removed to the park where the old clock tower was re-erected on top of a shelter made of brick walls and arches from the old Hall. Some Tuscan colonades from the inside of the Hall are also incorporated. The roots of the town's prosperity lay in the cloth industry, especially worsteds for suits, and Huddersfield cloth is still regarded as the world's finest. Ravensknowle House was a wealthy man's Italianate villa of 1860 and now houses the Tolson Memorial Museum which contains

The cloth hall clock-tower in Ravensknowle Park, Huddersfield.

material relating to Huddersfield's worsted cloth industry.

Our second clock tower is in the centre of Lindley, a suburb on the north-west perimeter of Huddersfield at the junction of Lidget Street and Aire Street (SE118/181). It is a square clock tower with an octagonal copper pagoda roof, originally built for the Sykes family by the remarkable Manchester arts and crafts architect Edgar Wood with sculptures by T. Stirling Lee. It is inscribed "This tower was erected by James Neild Sykes Esq. J. P. of Field Head, Lindley for the benefit of his native village in 1902".

Places of Interest in the Neighbourhood
68. Robin Hood's Grave (Brighouse)
69. Two Churchless Steeples (Mirfield)
73. "The Most Splendid Station Facade in England" (Huddersfield)
74. Four Thousand Years of History (Almondbury)

The spectacular railway station at Huddersfield.

73 "The Most Splendid Station Facade in England"

Position: Huddersfield (W. Yorks)
O. S. Map: Sheffield & Huddersfield Area Sheet: 110
Map Ref: SE143/168
Access: The railway station is in St. George's Square in the city centre.

So wrote John Betjeman of the railway station in Huddersfield. The great railway companies of the nineteenth-century often commissioned the construction of fine, gentlemanly buildings with grand facades in order to assure their fee-paying customers of the social respectability of travelling by rail.

The one at Huddersfield was designed by York architect J. P. Pritchett the Elder in 1847-48 and remains one of the finest early stations in England. Built in the Classical Corinthian style it has a facade 416 feet long dominated by a central, two-storey office block, entrance and refreshment room fronted by a magnificent eight-columned pediment portico, worthy of a Roman temple. The columns stand 68 feet high!

Flanking this are long colonnaded single-storey wings terminating in smaller 4-columned porticos. These each carry medallions with the coat of arms of the two railway companies responsible, namely the Lancashire and Yorkshire Railway and the Huddersfield and Manchester Railway and Canal Company. That no less than two companies should combine energies to produce such monumental architecture for what was at the time by no means the largest settlement in West Yorkshire may seem curious. In fact these two companies were originally hostile to each other while competing for the line's contract, but eventually came to a local agreement celebrated by the construction of a common station of the highest quality.

Places of Interest in the Neighbourhood
68. Robin Hood's Grave (Brighouse)
69. Two Churchless Steeples (Mirfield)
72. A Couple of Curious Clock Towers (Huddersfield)
74. Four Thousand Years of History (Almondbury)

74 Four Thousand Years of History

Position: Almondbury (W. Yorks)
O. S. Map: Sheffield & Huddersfield Area Sheet: 110
Map Ref: SE153/141
Access: The village of Almondbury is 1¼ miles south-east of Huddersfield and is dominated by the Castle Hill to the south-west.

Castle Hill is one of West Yorkshire's most important archaeological sites, although its most obvious feature, the Victorian Jubilee Tower, is its most recent structure (see back cover). This 900 feet high ridge commands impressive views down the Colne and Holme valleys and has natural defensive slopes on three sides. Excavations have shown that it was first occupied by Neolithic settlers c.2,000 BC who built an earth bank and ditch to defend themselves. From c.600 BC it was Iron Age settlers who developed the site as a fortress although a fire destroyed it a century later and it remained deserted until 1147 AD. At this time the Normans restored the earthworks in the form of a "motte-and-bailey" castle. During the latter part of the Norman occupation the castle was used as a hunting lodge and was finally demolished c.1340 AD. The hill also supported a beacon which was lit at the time of the Armada and was prepared in readiness for the expected invasion by Napoleon.

   A tavern was built on the hill in 1812 and was replaced by the current building in 1852, whilst the tower itself was erected by public subscription in 1899 at a cost of £3,398, to commemorate Victoria's Diamond Jubilee. The lantern on the top was also bought by public subscription for the Silver Jubilee of Queen Elizabeth II in 1977. The tower was restored in 1960 at a cost of £9,000 when its tower was reduced by 6 feet so that it was no longer at mountain height (1,000 feet), rather 996, 7 feet above sea level.

Places of Interest in the Neighbourhood
68. Robin Hood's Grave (Brighouse)
69. Two Churchless Steeples (Mirfield)
72. A Couple of Curious Clock Towers (Huddersfield)
73. "The Most Splendid Station Facade in England" (Huddersfield)
75. Three Great Floods (Holmfirth)

75 Three Great Floods

Position: Holmfirth (W. Yorks)
O. S. Map: Sheffield & Huddersfield Area Sheet: 110
Map Ref: SE14/08
Access: Holmfirth lies in the Holme Valley, 5 miles south of
Huddersfield on the A6024.

Holmfirth is almost surrounded by hills containing several large reservoirs. The streams from these hills, which converge in the Holme Valley, can be quickly swollen by storms or melting snow, presenting the threat of floods to the town further down. Three times Holmfirth has suffered tragedy as a result of this precarious geographical position. The first occasion was on Wednesday 23rd July, 1777 when a thunderstorm caused what was known for 100 years as "the Great Flood", claiming 3 lives. The height of the water is recorded on the wall of Wagstaff's Boot and Shoe shop in Station Road (SE142/082).

A row of gabled almshouses commemorates the second flood when the Bilberry Reservoir burst on 5th February, 1852 killing 81 people. Some 90 million gallons of water thundered down the valley and the

One of Holmfirth's three flood memorials.

extraordinary height of the water is recorded on a pillar in Towngate close to the bus station (SE142/082). The pillar had been erected much earlier in 1801 to mark the end of the war with France and the resulting Peace of Amiens, which brought with it a return of demand for locally produced textiles.

The final great flood occurred on Whit Monday, 1944 after a cloud burst had swollen the river to over 18 feet in parts. Three people drowned and 200 homes were flooded. A brass plaque recording the flood height is on the door of the "Elephant and Castle" inn, where Hollowgate joins Woodhead Road (SE144/085).

Holmfirth is better known today as the setting for the popular television series *Last of the Summer Wine* and as the home of Bamford's Postcard Museum.

Places of Interest in the Neighbourhood
74. Four Thousand Years of History (Almondbury)
77. The World's Largest Pie (Denby Dale)

Aerial photograph of the Norman iron pits at Bentley Grange (© British Crown copyright 1991/MOD reproduced with the permission of the Controller of Her Britannic Majesty's Stationery Office).

76 Where the Normans Dug for Iron

Position: Bentley Grange (W. Yorks)
O. S. Map: Sheffield & Huddersfield Area Sheet: 110
Map Ref: SE261/132
Access: Follow the A642 from Huddersfield to Wakefield for 6 miles,
then A637 to Flockton and down Church Lane to Emley. At a
T-junction turn eastwards towards West Bretton and 1 mile from Emley
the iron pits can be seen on either side of the road.

Norman monasteries were frequently given estates to cultivate by lay
benefactors. These "granges" were usually agricultural but at Bentley
Grange the estate was established to mine and process iron. The Cister-
cian monks of Byland Abbey, over 40 miles away, toiled long and hard
here in the second half of the twelfth century and, unusually, there are
considerable visible remains of their work. A series of pits was dug at
regular intervals and around these rose circular flat-topped mounds of
excavated waste. These so-called "bell-pits" were about 5 feet wide at
the top and opened out wider below, deep into the shale where nodules
of iron were to be found. The ore, once mined, was smelted in charcoal fuelled furnaces by the stream next to the wood. The stream itself
was dammed in order to turn a water wheel which provided power for
finishing the iron.

Forge and furnace slag litters the site. It is thought that up to 25
tons of iron were produced here each year representing a considerable
income for the monastery.

Places of Interest in the Neighbourhood
77. The World's Largest Pie (Denby Dale)
78. A Monster of a Barn (Gunthwaite)

77 The World's Largest Pie

Position: Denby Dale (W. Yorks)
O. S. Map: Sheffield & Huddersfield Area Sheet: 110
Map Ref: SE233/086
Access: Denby Dale lies about 7 miles west of Barnsley on the A635, and the Pie Hall is just outside the centre on the A636.

The village hall in Denby Dale is known locally as "Pie Hall" and contains much local history. In front of it is a flower bed planted in the world's largest pie dish, some 18 feet in length. On September 3rd, 1988, 100,000 people witnessed the baking of the ninth huge pie in Denby Dale celebrating the bicentenary of the baking of the first such pie. This had been baked in 1788 to celebrate the short-lived return to sanity of George III. It has been suggested that this form of celebration had been facilitated by the existence of large ovens for the local manufacture of earthenware pipes.

The second pie, in 1815, celebrated the defeat of Napoleon at Waterloo and a third even larger pie in 1846 commemorated the repeal of the Corn Laws. The table supporting the latter collapsed and the pie fell to the ground. It was suggested that this was a Tory plot to ruin the Liberals' celebration of the success of their M. P. s in bringing about the repeal. The next pie, to celebrate Queen Victoria's Golden Jubilee (1887), went bad and had to be buried in a nearby wood. Such was the catastrophe that funeral cards were printed and a "Resurrection Pie" appeared within a week!

The sixth pie in 1896 celebrated the jubilee of the Corn Law repeal and in 1928 the "Infirmary Pie" was baked to raise money to endow a bed in perpetuity at Huddersfield Royal Infirmary. The 1964 pie celebrated four royal births but was also known as the "Darby and Joan Pie" to raise funds for a community centre for local pensioners. It is the dish for this pie which is outside the village hall today. The most recent pie, in 1988, contained no less than 3,000 kilos of beef, 3,000 kilos of potatoes, and 700 kilos of onions!

Places of Interest in the Neighbourhood
75. Three Great Floods (Holmfirth)
76. Where the Normans Dug for Iron (Bentley Grange)
78. A Monster of a Barn (Gunthwaite)

78 A Monster of a Barn

Position: Gunthwaite (S. Yorks)
O. S. Map: Sheffield & Huddersfield Area Sheet: 110
Map Ref: SE238/066
Access: Take the A629, 2½ miles north out of Penistone, the B6115 to
Upper Denby and then a small track east into Gunthwaite Lane. The
barn is in a private farmyard at the bend in the road from where it can
be viewed. Permission to view the interior must be sought from the farm
and remember that it is filled with hay after August.

Gunthwaite is a hamlet with a Viking name. A French family, the
Bosvilles, inherited Gunthwaite Hall in 1375 from the family of that
name, but it unfortunately burned down in the nineteenth century.
However, the massive sixteenth-century manorial tithe barn for the
collection of tithes remains in the grounds. Of cruck or king-post truss
pattern, the timber-frame barn is probably the biggest tithe barn in
England and certainly one of the finest. South-west Yorkshire is famous

The sixteenth-century tithe barn at Gunthwaite.

for the profusion of its cruck-built structures, but one has to look hard for them as they are more readily recognisable from the interior than the outside.

The barn is around 160 by 45 feet in size and 30 feet high, with 3 threshing floors. It was probably built by Godfrey Bosville around 1550. It features 10 king-post roof trusses, supported on pillars standing on stone bases, 11 bays, 3 wagon entrances and a pegged roof with stone slates. Local tradition speaks of a carpenter's apprentice who spent all his apprenticeship solely making pegs! That it is decorative as well as utilitarian is suggested by the herringbone framing along the top of the walls. It still serves as a store though it is now used jointly by two farms.

Also of interest is a well-preserved, paved packhorse causeway joining the hamlets of Gunthwaite and Cat Hill with the church and market at Penistone.

Places of Interest in the Neighbourhood
76. Where the Normans Dug for Iron (Bentley Grange)
77. The World's Largest Pie (Denby Dale)

79 This Forge is the Tops!

Position: Wortley (S. Yorks)
O. S. Map: Sheffield & Huddersfield Area Sheet: 110
Map Ref: SK294/999
Access: Wortley lies between Deepcar and Thurgoland just off the A629, 8 miles north-west of Sheffield from where the forge is signposted. It is open on Sundays 11. 00 am – 5. 00 pm and there are occasional working days.

The top forge at Wortley Ironworks is curious because it is now the sole surviving "in situ" water-driven iron forge in Britain, complete with dam, sluices and water wheels. It dates from the early seventeenth century and was respectively in the hands of Sir Francis Wortley (c1620), the Spencers (after the Civil War), the Andrews Family (1850-1907) and finally the Wortley Iron Company (1907-1912). It has no less than 3 water wheels and two hammers and produced wrought iron from 1620-1912. The second water wheel and forge hammer were eighteenth-century additions and the helve hammer and cranes date from the nineteenth-century. Originally the forge made iron for nails and cannon balls (see no. 23) but later rod and bar iron, and eventually railway axles with the advent of railways.

There is a unique collection of early stationary steam engines in the foundry as well as working exhibits illustrating the smith's craft in the Blacksmith's shop. The site has been painstakingly restored by the Sheffield Trades Historical Society.

Places of Interest in the Neighbourhood
23. Cannon Balls and a Curious Custom (Tankersley)
24. A Memorial within a Memorial (Barnsley)
80. The Rival Folly Builders (Hood Green)
81. A Blast from the Past! (Birdwell)
82. Evidence of Body-snatchers (Bradfield)

The Steeple Lodge gatehouse at Wentworth Castle.

80 The Rival Folly Builders

Position: Hood Green (S. Yorks)
O. S. Map: Sheffield & Huddersfield Area Sheet: 110
Map Ref: SE320/033
Access: Leave the M1 At junction 36, pass through Birdwell and follow
Rockley Lane below the motorway and then Wentworth Castle estate
lies between the villages of Stainborough and Hood Green.

The many follies and monuments on the estates of Wentworth Castle
and Wentworth Woodhouse (see no. 8) to some extent reflect a bit-
ter rivalry between the owners of these great South Yorkshire country
homes.

When Sir William Wentworth of Wakefield died in 1695, the heir to
the Wentworth Woodhouse estate was not his son Thomas Wentworth,
great nephew of Sir Thomas Wentworth, first earl of Strafford, but his
nephew Thomas Watson. Thomas Wentworth (1672-1739), a Tory who
had amassed a fortune in the army and as a diplomat, was furious and
bought Stainborough Hall at Hood Green, a mere 7 miles away. He
immediately set about adding a new wing to the house and building
follies designed to outshine his Whig cousin's at Wentworth Woodhouse. On a hill to the west he built a mock ruin in 1734 called
Stainborough Castle (SE316/031). This was made up of 4 towers representing himself and his three daughters but is unfortunately not accessible to the public. Visible, however, is the main entrance to the house
which is dominated by the Steeple Lodge (SE319/036), a gate-house
disguised as a Gothic church complete with pinnacled tower and castellated cottage attached. In 1731 Wentworth, by now the Earl of Strafford, re-named his superior house Wentworth Castle. When the Earl
died in 1739, William Wentworth inherited, adding a further wing to the
house in 1759-64. He also continued the folly tradition by building an
obelisk near Stainborough Castle which commemorates a neighbour,
Lady Mary Wortley Montague, who introduced the smallpox vaccine
to this country. An earlier obelisk erected in 1734 to Queen Anne is
visible from Rockley Lane (SE332/029). Yet another was added in 1775
at Birdwell (SE348/007) giving directions to the house.

Unfortunately, now inaccessible or lost are the column to Minerva
(1743) in memory of William's father-in-law, the Classical building
(1756) at Rockley Woodhouse, a copy of Chichester's Market cross
(1759), various sham fortifications, a pyramid and a Chinese temple.

Although the follies at Wentworth Woodhouse are now more famous,

Wentworth Castle, now a college, can lay claim to South Yorkshire's only Grade One listed garden. Founded in 1672 it is world famous for its rhododendrons grown from seeds collected by Victorian gentleman explorers in the Far East (Viewing is by appointment only – phone Barnsley 235426, although the gardens are open on August Bank Holiday).

Places of Interest in the Neighbourhood
8. Follies Fit for a King (Wentworth)
23. Cannon Balls and a Curious Custom (Tankersley)
24. A Memorial within a Memorial (Barnsley)
25. Monuments to Brave Miners (Barnsley)
79. This Forge is the Tops! (Wortley)
81. A Blast from the Past! (Birdwell)

The seventeenth-century Rockley Furnace near Birdwell.

81 A Blast from the Past!

Position: Birdwell (S. Yorks)
O. S. Map: Sheffield & Huddersfield Area Sheet: 110
Map Ref: SE338/026
Access: Leave the M1 at Junction 36, passing through Birdwell and turn left below the motorway onto Rockley Lane. Rockley furnace is signposted down a track but remember to turn right at the gate.

Rockley furnace is Europe's oldest surviving charcoal blast furnace. Remarkably it dates from 1652 and was built by Lionel Copley, a Rotherham man. At one time it would have produced up to 400 tons of pig iron per annum and required 1,000-1,200 horse loads of charcoal for fuel. Most of the latter came from coppiced woods up to 15 miles away. Industrial sites in relatively pastoral settings tend to survive and this is no exception set, as it is, in a wooded hollow close to a stream and ironstone workings.

Some excavations have taken place in recent years revealing the wheel pit, bellows building, casting pit and the stone charging bank. Some traces of the dams have been traced in the surrounding woodland.

The furnace ceased production in the mid eighteenth-century, although it re-opened briefly during the Napoleonic Wars.

Places of Interest in the Neighbourhood
23. Cannon Balls and a Curious Custom (Tankersley)
24. A Memorial within a Memorial (Barnsley)
25. Monuments to Brave Miners (Barnsley)
79. This Forge is the Tops! (Wortley)
80. The Rival Folly Builders (Hood Green)

82 Evidence of Body-snatchers

Position: Bradfield (S. Yorks)
O. S. Map: Sheffield & Huddersfield Area Sheet: 110
Map Ref: SK266/926
Access: The village of Bradfield lies 6 miles north-west of Sheffield on the B6077 in the scenic Loxley Valley.

The pretty village is divided into Upper and Lower Bradfield. The fine church of St. Nicholas in the former contains a brass plaque showing John Morewood with his wife and fifteen children! More curious, however, is the small turret-like building in the churchyard. This is in fact a watch-house built in 1745 to house look-outs who protected the cemetery from body-snatchers. It was once a macabre, profitable and illegal business stealing corpses to sell to surgeons and hospitals.

Places of Interest in the Neighbourhood
79. This Forge is the Tops! (Wortley)

The body-snatcher's watchhouse at Upper Bradfield.

Index

Places by page number

The Curiosities of England

The following titles in the series have already been published and can be ordered at all bookshops, or in case of difficulties direct from the publishers.

Cheshire Curiosities Peter Bamford 0 946159 96 3

Cotswold Curiosities Reginald Dixon 0 946159 51 1

Dorset Curiosities George Osborn 0 946159 38 6

East Anglian Curiosities Rick O'Brien 0 946159 97 1

Hampshire Curiosities Jo Draper 0 946159 57 2

Hertfordshire Curiosities John Lucas 0 946159 75 0

Isle of Wight Curiosities Jack Jones 0 946159 67 X

Kent Curiosities John Vigar 0 946159 95 5

Nottinghamshire Curiosities Geoffrey Oldfield 0 946159 98 X

Somerset Curiosities Enid Byford 0 946159 48 3

South and West Yorkshire Curiosities Duncan & Trevor Smith
0 946159 99 8